SpringerBriefs in Computer Science

SpringerBriefs present concise summaries of cutting-edge research and practical applications across a wide spectrum of fields. Featuring compact volumes of 50 to 125 pages, the series covers a range of content from professional to academic.

Typical topics might include:

- A timely report of state-of-the art analytical techniques
- A bridge between new research results, as published in journal articles, and a contextual literature review
- A snapshot of a hot or emerging topic
- An in-depth case study or clinical example
- A presentation of core concepts that students must understand in order to make independent contributions

Briefs allow authors to present their ideas and readers to absorb them with minimal time investment. Briefs will be published as part of Springer's eBook collection, with millions of users worldwide. In addition, Briefs will be available for individual print and electronic purchase. Briefs are characterized by fast, global electronic dissemination, standard publishing contracts, easy-to-use manuscript preparation and formatting guidelines, and expedited production schedules. We aim for publication 8-12 weeks after acceptance. Both solicited and unsolicited manuscripts are considered for publication in this series.

More information about this series at http://www.springer.com/series/10028

Borko Furht • Esad Akar
Whitney Angelica Andrews

Digital Image Processing: Practical Approach

 Springer

Borko Furht
Department of Computer & Electrical
Engineering and Computer Science
Florida Atlantic University
Boca Raton, FL, USA

Esad Akar
Department of Computer & Electrical
Engineering and Computer Science
Florida Atlantic University
Boca Raton, FL, USA

Whitney Angelica Andrews
Department of Computer & Electrical
Engineering and Computer Science
Florida Atlantic University
Boca Raton, FL, USA

ISSN 2191-5768   ISSN 2191-5776 (electronic)
SpringerBriefs in Computer Science
ISBN 978-3-319-96633-5   ISBN 978-3-319-96634-2 (eBook)
https://doi.org/10.1007/978-3-319-96634-2

Library of Congress Control Number: 2018952345

This Springer imprint is published by the registered company Springer Nature Switzerland AG
The registered company address is: Gewerbestrasse 11, 6330 Cham, Switzerland

Preface

This book is intended for beginners in the field who would like to understand the basic concepts of digital image processing and apply them in programming some fundamental digital image processing algorithms. It is our assumption that the reader has some background in programming including the basics of C and C++. The book is of practical nature, and the fundamental concepts of image processing discussed in each chapter are showcased with demo programs. The reader is encouraged to understand and run these programs as well as create similar programs proposed in the book.

The book consists of ten chapters. The book begins with the introduction to image concept, classification of images, and various image formats. Then, it follows up with Chaps. 2 and 3 on creating user interface and image loading and rendering. After successfully completing and understanding these concepts, the reader will be able to begin writing basic programs in image processing. In Chaps. 4 and 5, we introduce some relatively simple image processing techniques, such as creating image histograms and detecting changes in colors and present programs that accomplish these techniques. Chapters 6 and 7 introduce more complex image processing problems and their solutions including lossless image compression and similarity-based image retrieval.

When completing these chapters and related programming examples, the reader will be able to understand and write some exciting image processing applications. Lastly, Chaps. 8, 9, and 10 present three applications including how to hide data in digital images, how to create a transition from one to another image, and how to embed one image into another image with resizing. Chapters 11, 12, and 13 were completed by students as part of Introduction to Image and Video Processing class at Florida Atlantic University taught in Spring 2018.

The book can be used as a practical textbook for basic courses on image processing. The main features of the book can be summarized as follows:

1. The book describes the basic concept of digital image processing.
2. The focus of the book is practical programming examples of fundamental image processing algorithms.
3. Link to complete programs allows readers to run, test programs, and design various image processing solutions. The libraries used in this book can be found at https://github.com/scarface382/libraries, and source code for all programs described in the book can be found at http://github.com/scarface382/multimedia-examples.

Boca Raton, FL, USA   Borko Furht
2018   Esad Akar
                                                           Whitney Angelica Andrews

Contents

Chapter 1
Introduction to Digital Imaging

1.1 Image Concept

Image is a two-dimensional array of samples or pixels, as illustrated in Fig. 1.1.

Each pixel consists of number of bits. Based on number of bits per pixel, Table 1.1 classifies images into four categories: binary, computer graphics, grayscale, and color images. Digital images come in different flavors. Images can be made up pixels that are either fully black or fully white, called binary images. Grayscale images contains pixels where the pixel color values vary between a range of black, grey, and white. Color images can capture pixel values of any color such as red, blue, and green.

In this book, we will focus on color and grayscale images. The most common representation of color images, RGB representation (Red, Green, Blue) is based on trichromatic theory that the sensation of color is produced by selectively exciting three classes of receptors in the eye. Figure 1.2 shows the three-dimensional representation of color images consisting of these three components: R, G, and B.

In 24-bit color format, each color is represented with 8 bits. Therefore, the elements in the three-dimensional cube have values from (0,0,0) to (255,255,255). Black color is defined as (0,0,0) and the white component as (255,255,255). Grayscale image is defined as the straight line in the three-dimensional cube, which is when $R = G = B$.

The term channel in the context of digital images refers to number of color components used to display a pixel value. A three-channel image simply means a RGB color image. Pixels of grayscale images can be represented with a single value so they are single channel images. RGBA images which stand for Red, Green, Blue, Alpha are regular RGB images with a fourth channel called the alpha channel which controls the transparency level of the pixels. In most digital image editing software, layers of image objects can be stacked together. By tweaking the transparency/opacity levels of these layers, the bottom layer can be made to show through as seen in Fig. 1.3. Of course, when the final design is exported as a regular image file,

© The Author(s), under exclusive licence to Springer Nature Switzerland AG 2018
B. Furht et al., *Digital Image Processing: Practical Approach*, SpringerBriefs in
Computer Science, https://doi.org/10.1007/978-3-319-96634-2_1

Fig. 1.1 Image concept
(5 × 5 pixels)

3	78	98	178	9
12	0	255	11	254
75	23	95	85	0
66	98	10	56	74
65	02	35	74	89

Table 1.1 Image
classification based on number
of bits per pixel

Image type	Number of bits/pixel
Binary image	1
Computer graphics	4
Grayscale image	8
Color image	16–24

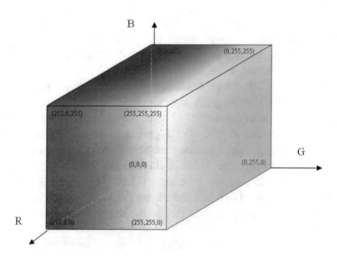

Fig. 1.2 Three-dimensional representation of color images using R, G, and B components

the layer information is not stored so the areas where the layers overlap are forced in a single stream of pixels instead of two. In applications such as Internet browsers that render images to the screen, images with RGBA channels inform the application how the image should be displayed when it is displayed over any background image e.g. a solid background color or another image.

Digital cameras typically contain filters with three sensors for each color component in RGB. The light source captured by the lenses is processed through the color

Fig. 1.3 An image layer with different levels of opacity

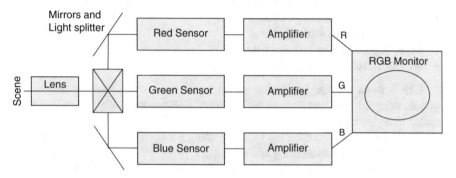

Fig. 1.4 Three-sensor RGB color video camera and TGB monitor

filter, which produces RGB component values for every pixel. The captured RGB values then can be displayed using a RGB monitor as illustrated in Fig. 1.4.

Another color model often used in digital image and video processing is UYV color model, which describes color perception and consists of one luminance component (Y) and two chrominance components (U and V). The YUV image representation can be created from RGB presentation using the following approximate mathematical description:

$$Y = 0.3R + 0.6G + 0.1B$$

$$V = R - Y$$

$$U = B - Y$$

The YUV color model consists of a luminance component Y, which captures the brightness of the pixel, and two chrominance components, U and V, that capture color information.

When $R = G = B$ then $Y = R = G = B$, which is a grayscale image. In summary, to convert a full color RGB image into a grayscale image, the following approximate formula can be used:

$$Y = 0.3R + 0.6G + 0.1B$$

This formula will be used in subsequent chapters when dealing with grayscale images.

1.2   Image File Formats

In this section we introduce several common image file formats:

- GIF: Graphics Interchange Format (limited to 8-bit color images)
- JPEG: Standard for image compression
- PNG: Portable Network Graphics
- TIFF: Tagged Image File Format
- Windows BMP (BitMap) format

GIF is most suitable for storing graphics with few colors, such as simple diagrams, shapes, logos, and cartoon style images. GIF supports only 256 colors and a single transparent color.

JPEG images are compressed typically using a lossy compression method. The format is dominantly used in digital cameras.

PNG file format is a free, open-source alternative to GIF. The PNG file format supports eight-bit paletted images and 24-bit truecolor (16 million colors).

TIFF image format is a flexible format that normally saves eight bits or sixteen bits per color (red, green, blue) for 24-bit and 48-bit totals, respectively.

Windows BMP handles graphic files within the Microsoft Windows OS. Typically, BMP files are uncompressed, and therefore large and lossless; their advantage is their simple structure and wide acceptance in Windows programs.

1.3   Image Resolution

As we already discussed, an image is defined using pixels. The resolution (R) defines the total number of pixels in an image as:

$$R = n \times m$$

where n specifies the number of pixels in horizontal direction, and m in vertical direction. If the total number of pixels is large than the quality of the image is higher, and the memory to store the image and the time to transmit the image will be higher as well. Typical image resolutions are shown in Table 1.2. The table also shows the total number of pixels for each resolution as well as memory needed to save the full color image.

Table 1.2 Image resolutions

Type of image/video	Resolution	Number of pixels	Memory
VGA	640 × 480	307,200	921,600 B
NTSC, DVD	720 × 480	345,600	1.036 MB
Super VGA	1024 × 768	786,432	2.305 MB
HD DVD, Blu-ray	1280 × 720	921,600	2.764 MB
HDV	1920 × 1080	2,073,600	6.22 MB
4K UHDTV	3840 × 2160	8,294,400	24.883 MB
8K UHDTV	7680 × 4320	33,177,600	99.532 MB
16K Digital cinema	15360 × 8640	132,710,400	398.131 MB
64K Digital cinema	61440 × 34560	2.12×10^9	6.37 GB

Here are two examples of calculating the number of pixels and the memory for two types of images:

(a) For a 640 × 480 VGA pixel image with 240 bit color, the number of pixels is 640 × 480 = 307,200 pixels. The memory required to store the image is:
   M = 307,200 pixels × 3 bytes = 921,600 bytes = 921.600 KB
(b) For a high-definition image 1920 × 1800, the number of pixels is 1920 × 1800 = 2,073,600 pixels, and the required memory to store the image is:
   M = 2,073,600 pixels × 3 bytes = 6,220,000 bytes = 6.22 MB

In this chapter we discussed the basics of digital images. Digital images are composed of pixels where different color models, such as RGB and YUV, can be used to represent color values.

Chapter 2
Creating User Interface

Every chapter in this book includes a demo program to explain the material, the theory behind digital image topics, and provides code that the reader can run and manipulate. Instead of writing command line demo programs with little user interaction, we opted to write programs with a User Interface (UI) that includes essential UI elements such as buttons, sliders, and ability to display images on the screen. Thus, in this chapter, we present the UI library we have chosen to use and how to use it in the context of the digital image programming.

The UI library we selected for all the projects is **ImGui,** which is an open-source library written in C++ with MIT license. ImGui is defined on its GitHub page as a bloat-free graphical user interface library for C++. It outputs optimized vertex buffers that you can render anytime in your 3D-pipeline enabled application and can be found at http://github.com/ocornut/imgui.

ImGui is different than the traditional UI C++ libraries. The internals of ImGui resembles a state-machine instead. There are no classes for each UI class objects such as a button, a text box, a window, etc. There is no need to create separate files for UI code or the main logic code. Each function resides in the ImGui namespace and the order of objects to be rendered are dictated by the order of function calls made. A bit more experience with graphics programing is needed, however, to be able to use it. There exists no framework that renders the vertex buffers ImGui creates, so the programmer needs to create a window context, initialize graphics libraries (OpenGL in our case), and write the code for transferring user input such as key strokes and mouse clicks over to ImGui for processing. For OpenGL initialization, we use the GLEW library.

For creating a window and processing user input, we make use of GLFW, another useful wrapper library. To learn more about GLEW and GLFW, visit glew.sourceforge.net and glfw.org. The maintainers of ImGui have already provided a full implementation that uses GLEW and GLFW so we made use of that. To observe how ImGui interacts with GFLW, read imgui_glfw.h and observe how user input is processed and vertex buffers are rendered in the graphics pipeline.

© The Author(s), under exclusive licence to Springer Nature Switzerland AG 2018
B. Furht et al., *Digital Image Processing: Practical Approach*, SpringerBriefs in Computer Science, https://doi.org/10.1007/978-3-319-96634-2_2

Fig. 2.1 User interface
example: outcome of the
program

All the code for UI is inside the main 'forever' loop featured in the code text box. ImGui gives the ability to create multiple windows inside one OS windows. Windows and groups are created by making begin and end calls. To create a new ImGui window, a call to ImGui::Begin(...) is made. Next, any UI object is created by calling the necessary function. A button with label 'click me' simply requires ImGui::Button("click me") call. When a user click on that button, the function returns true, so putting the ImGui::Button(...) call in an if statement lets the programmer write the code for the button click event. Once all objects are put into the rendering list by their respective ImGui calls, a final ImGui::End() call is made. At the end of the main loop, ImGui::Render() is called, buffers are switched, rendered, and put to the screen.

We present next a simple example program. With the help of glfw, glew, and ImGui libraries, the program creates an UI window, which contains a single button and a text area. Each time the user clicks the button, the number is incremented in the text area; refer to Fig. 2.1.

The function calls between the start of main and the while loop initializes GLFW and GLEW libraries and creates an OS window that we can use to render our UI. The while-loop will run forever as long as the user does not close the window. If a terminate message makes it way from the OS to the GLFW context, the glfwWindowShouldClose(window) statement will return true, end the while loop, initiate cleanup, and terminate the program.

At the start of the loop once user input is polled with glfwPollEvents() and ImGui is informed that a new frame is being rendered with ImGui_ImplGlfwGL3_NewFrame(), we can begin calling the necessary UI functions for window display. In this example, we create a window that includes a button and a text area that displays the current x value. The x value initially has a value of zero, but with each click of the button, the value of x is incremented by one. To render our UI components to the screen, we call a few more functions. After fetching the OS window size, we tell OpenGL to clear the screen with the already defined vector clear_color. Then, ImGui::Render() renders whatever UI component function we previously called (ImGui window, button, text, etc.) and glfwSwapBuffers (window) makes the changes on the screen. This pattern of library initialization, loop, and cleanup is present throughout all the projects in the following chapters. The program shown next includes library initializations, main loop, ImGui calls, and rendering.

```
// UI example code
// ImGui headers
#include <image.h>
#include <imgui/local.h>

int main()
{
    // Setup window
    glfwSetErrorCallback(error_callback);
    if (!glfwInit())
        return 1;

    // OpenGl version 3
    glfwWindowHint(GLFW_CONTEXT_VERSION_MAJOR, 3);
    glfwWindowHint(GLFW_CONTEXT_VERSION_MINOR, 3);
    glfwWindowHint(GLFW_OPENGL_PROFILE, GLFW_OPENGL_CORE_PROFILE);

    // Create Window and init glew
    GLFWwindow* window = glfwCreateWindow(950,500, "Demo 1", NULL, NULL);
    glfwMakeContextCurrent(window);
    glewInit();

    // Setup ImGui binding
    ImGui_ImplGlfwGL3_Init(window, true);

    ImVec4 clear_color = ImColor(114, 144, 154);
    int x = 0;

    // main loop
    while (!glfwWindowShouldClose(window)) {

        // user events such as clicking, typing, and moving cursor
        glfwPollEvents();
        ImGui_ImplGlfwGL3_NewFrame();

        // UI components
        ImGui::Begin("any window title");
        if (ImGui::Button("CLICK ME"))
            x++;
        ImGui::Text("X: %d", x);
        ImGui::End();

        // window size
        int display_w, display_h;
        glfwGetFramebufferSize(window, &display_w, &display_h);

        // clear the screen
        glViewport(0, 0, display_w, display_h);
        glClearColor(clear_color.x, clear_color.y, clear_color.z,
            clear_color.w);
        glClear(GL_COLOR_BUFFER_BIT);

        // finally render
        ImGui::Render();
        glfwSwapBuffers(window);
    }
    // Cleanup
    ImGui_ImplGlfwGL3_Shutdown();
    glfwTerminate();
}
```

2.1 Compiling the Program

For every chapter in this book, we have written one or two demo programs in C++ to go along with the explanation of each topic. To successfully compile and run each program, let us discuss the steps of acquiring a C++ compiler, libraries we used, and the source code for the demo programs. The programs were compiled using Windows 7, 9 and 10 so if you are running Linux or MacOS checkout the GitHub repository of ImGui for instructions on how to compile on these platforms.

The source code for the demo programs can be found on GitHub by downloading the repository (github.com/scarface382/multimedia-examples). You can unzip the file in any location in your computer. Each folder corresponds to a chapter in this book and contains the files for the source code and a makefile which contains information of where libraries are located and what compiler flags needs to be passed on to the compiler. Here is the content of the makefile for this chapter:

```
LIBDIR = C:/libraries/lib
LIB = -L $(LIBDIR) -lOpenGL32
DLL = $(LIBDIR)/libglew32.dll.a $(LIBDIR)/libglfw3dll.a

INC = C:/libraries/include
IMGUI = $(INC)/imgui/imgui.cpp $(INC)/imgui/imgui_draw.cpp

all:
        g++ -std=c++11 main.cpp $(IMGUI) -I $(INC) $(DLL) $(LIB) -o demo
```

The library repository, which includes ImGui, GLEW, GLFW, and the utility functions, are used in the demo programs and can be found at (https://github.com/scarface382/libraries). Make sure to download and move the content of this repository to C:/libraries.

To make installing both g++ and make programs easier for you, we've also included an installation application mingw-w64-install in the libraries repository. When you run the installation, make sure that you select x_86 architecture if your computer has a 64-bit architecture (almost all new computers do) under installation settings. For the destination folder, install everything under C:/mingw. Once you are done with installation, rename mingw32-make.exe to make.exe under C:/mingw/mingw64/bin. This is so that we don't have to keep typing mingw32-make every time we want to run a makefile script to compile a program.

At this point, we have acquired our compiler, source code, and all the necessary libraries but we are not ready to compile the code yet. We need to add the path of our libraries folder and the location of our compiler and make program to the global environment variables of Windows so that when we compile by running make in the console, the make program along with g++ can be located. To add these paths, simply run these two commands in your console ran as administrator:

```
setx /M path "C:\libraries\lib;%path%"
```

```
setx /M path " C:\mingw\mingw64\bin;%path%"
```

Finally, we are ready to compile. Open a new console and change working directory to the directory of the demo program for first chapter then run:

```
make
```

The code should be compiled by g++ and it should output a new executable with the name 'demo.exe'.

We have discussed the UI library that we used in demo programs and how to acquire and compile the source code for all the chapters. In the next chapter we discuss how images are decoded, loaded, and rendered.

Chapter 3
Image Loading and Rendering

3.1 Loading Image from Disk

JPEG and PNG are some of the most popular digital image file types. Pixel values are compressed with some form of compression in these file, and as a result it is not possible to open a digital image file and directly read the pixel values. The image must be first be decoded, which returns the decompressed pixel values along with other necessary information such as image resolution. For this task, we use stb_image.h written by Sean Barrett which is an image loader library that can decode images and extract pixel values from JPEG and PNG files (https://github.com/nothings/stb).

To handle image files with ease in accordance with this library, we use the struct definition below for all loaded image files:

```
typedef uint8_t uint8;

struct Image
{
    uint8* pixels = NULL; // 8-bit unsigned integer
    GLuint texture;
    int texture_loaded = 0;
    int width;
    int height;
    int n; //number of color channels, can be 3 (RGB) or 4 (RGBA)
};
```

This definition contains all the information of an image that we need: the pixel value, the texture, the width, the height, and the number of color channels. The struct allows easy access to the images attributes which is especially convenient when handling multiple images at the same time.

© The Author(s), under exclusive licence to Springer Nature Switzerland AG 2018
B. Furht et al., *Digital Image Processing: Practical Approach*, SpringerBriefs in
Computer Science, https://doi.org/10.1007/978-3-319-96634-2_3

stb_image.h is a single header file that contains all the functions that we need. Include this header file at the start of any program, with this macro definition:

```
#define STB_IMAGE_IMPLEMENTATION
#include <stb/stb_image.h>
```

The #define tells stb_image.h that we want access to the functions and not just function definitions that is located at the top of the file. The function we use the most from that library is stbi_load. See the following textbox for an example.

```
// image filename is 'cat.png'
#define RGBA 4
Image a;
a.pixels = (uint8*)stbi_load("cat.png", &a.height, &a.width, &a.n, RGBA);
```

The stbi_load function returns a 'unsinged char *' which points to a sequence of memory that contains pixel values. The function also writes to the height, the width, and the number of color components the image is made up of (RGB, or RGBA) to the appropriate struct members. In this case, a.n is the number of channels. We specifically request an RGBA output by passing 'RGBA' as the last parameter. Each unsigned char in memory is a color component value. If the image that is loaded an RGBA image, then the number of color components is four, and four sequential RGBA values make up one pixel. An RGBA image that is 10 pixels by 10 pixels contains 400 uint8 (unsinged char) color components (10 * 10 * 4) where each row in the image contains 40 colors components. Here is sample code that changes each R color component to the value 112.

```
int length = a.height * a.width * RGBA;
for (int i=0; i < length; i+= RGBA) {
        a.pixels[i]   = 112;
}

// do other work with the pixels

free(a.pixels); // cleanup
```

Notice that we increment i by 4 to skip GBA values and access R values. To clean up the memory allocated by stbi_load, you can simply call free(a.pixels) or stbi_image_free(a.pixels) to be fully compliant with stb.

3.2   Writing to Disk

Loading the image file to memory is necessary if we need to make changes to it, such as making each R component 112 in the previous example. After manipulation, the image may be saved to disk using another stb library: stb_image_write.h. Here is the sample code:

```
#define STB_IMAGE_WRITE_IMPLEMENTATION
#include <stb/stb_image_write.h>

stbi_write_png("cat_manipulated.png", a.width, a.height, RGBA, a.pixels,0);
```

3.3   Creating Texture from Images

Images can be loaded from the disk to memory using a few lines of code. The next step is to render them to screen. Since UI rendering is done directly with OpenGL under ImGui, the loaded image needs to be converted to an OpenGL texture. We have provided a function texture_image() in imgui/local.h file that generates an image texture given an Image struct. Observe that in the Image struct, there are two texture related members: texture and texture_loaded. These members are filled out with the necessary texture information to pass onto ImGui for rendering. The following example creates an ImGui window, loads, and displays an image the user has selected from their computer by click "Select Image" button, as illustrated in Fig. 3.1.

Fig. 3.1 Creating 'Select Image' button and loading an image

```
// header files, main function, and library initialization

while (!glfwWindowShouldClose(window))
{
    glfwPollEvents();
    ImGui_ImplGlfwGL3_NewFrame();

    ImGui::Begin("Slider Window");
    if (a.texture_loaded)
        ImGui::Image((void*)a.texture, resize_ui(a.width, a.height, 300));

    if (ImGui::Button("Select Image"))
        ImGui::OpenPopup("select 0");

    std::string tmp = image_select(0); //opens the file list

    if (tmp != "") {
        reset_image(&a);
        a.pixels = stbi_load(tmp.c_str(), &a.width, &a.height, &a.n, RGBA);
        texture_image(&a);
        free_image(&a);
    }
    ImGui::End();

    // Gl Rendering
    int display_w, display_h;
    glfwGetFramebufferSize(window, &display_w, &display_h);
    glViewport(0, 0, display_w, display_h);
    glClearColor(clear_color.x, clear_color.y, clear_color.z, clear_color.w);
    glClear(GL_COLOR_BUFFER_BIT);
    ImGui::Render();
    glfwSwapBuffers(window);
}
// cleanup...
```

Note that in the code section, we have skipped important steps such as including header files, writing the main function, creating the window, polling input, writing the rendering, and the cleanup code. Without the inclusion of those components the program will not compile (see the previous UI chapter for examples and explanations for those components). As always, you can examine the code in the source file we have written for this chapter.

When the image selection button is clicked, image_select() function is called and a pop up with a list of files in the directory of the executable file opens. The user can navigate through the folders and go up one directory by clicking the ".." at the top of the list. Once a file is selected, the name of the file is returned and is passed to stbi_load() for image file loading.

The function call ImGui::Image((void*)a.texture, ImVec2(a.width, a.height)), as shown in the previous example, takes two parameters: the first being the texture and the second being the image size in the form of a ImGui vector with just a x and a y component. The image size controls how large the image will be displayed on the screen. We discuss actual resizing, not just UI resizing, in Chap. 10.

3.4 Converting Color to Grayscale Images

Now that we've shown how to load and render an image, let's discuss the details of coding the simple image processing task of converting color images to grayscale. As we discussed in Chap. 1, to convert a color pixel to a grayscale, we need to apply the luminance value of the pixel to every component in RGB using this formula:

$$Y = 0.3R + 0.6G + 0.1B$$

The program written for this section works the same as the previous ImGui but it displays a second, grayscale image next to the original when the user selects an image, as can be seen in Fig. 3.2.

Fig. 3.2 Example of converting the color to the grayscale image

```
while (!glfwWindowShouldClose(window))
{
    glfwPollEvents();
    ImGui_ImplGlfwGL3_NewFrame();

    ImGui::Begin("Slider Window");

    if (a.texture_loaded && b.texture_loaded) {
        ImGui::Image((void*)a.texture, resize_ui(a.width, a.height, 300));
        ImGui::SameLine();
        ImGui::Image((void*)b.texture, resize_ui(b.width, b.height, 300));
    }

    if (ImGui::Button("Select Image"))
        ImGui::OpenPopup("select 0");

    std::string tmp = image_select(0); //opens the file list and assigns to tmp

    if (tmp != "") {
        reset_image(&a);
        reset_image(&b);
        a.pixels = stbi_load(tmp.c_str(), &a.width, &a.height, &a.n, RGBA);
        texture_image(&a);

        // allocate new memory for grayscale image and convert image to grayscale
        int length = a.width * a.height * RGBA;
        b.pixels = (uint8*)malloc(length);
        b.width = a.width;
        b.height = a.height;
        b.n = a.n;

        for (int i=0; i < length; i+= RGBA) {

            float R = a.pixels[i];
            float G = a.pixels[i+1];
            float B = a.pixels[i+2];
            float A = a.pixels[i+3];

            int Y = (0.3 * R) + (0.6 * G) + (0.1 * B);

            b.pixels[i] = Y;
            b.pixels[i+1] = Y;
            b.pixels[i+2] = Y;
            b.pixels[i+3] = A;
        }
        texture_image(&b);
    }
}
```

```
ImGui::End();

// Gl Rendering
int display_w, display_h;
glfwGetFramebufferSize(window, &display_w, &display_h);
glViewport(0, 0, display_w, display_h);
glClearColor(clear_color.x, clear_color.y, clear_color.z, clear_color.w);
glClear(GL_COLOR_BUFFER_BIT);
ImGui::Render();
glfwSwapBuffers(window);
}
```

The code for this program is an extension to the previous demo. Just as before, when an image file is selected, the image is loaded and is given a new to texture which is used to render the image. The next part is new and handles the allocation of enough memory for the grayscale image and the conversion to grayscale of the loaded image. The 'for loop' iterates over every color component of the original image and access each RGBA component of every pixel. Next, the luminance Y value is computed and assigned to each color component of the grayscale image. At the end of the loop, a texture is created for the grayscale image which gets rendered in the next iteration of the while loop under the very first if statement.

By knowing how to load and display image file in our UI programs, we are now ready to discuss more topics and ideas on digital image processing and write programs to put these ideas to the test.

Chapter 4
Creating Image Histograms

In this chapter, we discuss the basics on how to create color histograms for images. A histogram is a graphical representation of the number of pixels in an image. As an example, assume a 10×6 pixel image shown in Fig. 4.1. The pixels are one-byte data, and their values are between 0 and 255. The histogram for this simple image is shown in Fig. 4.2.

Color histogram is a representation of the distribution of colors in an image. To calculate the frequency of each color component, we simply increment a counter for every RGB component value between 0 and 255. All we need is three arrays of size 256 indexes. We iterate over each component in RGB and using the component value as the index, we increment the counter in the array. You can observe how to do this in code excerpt below:

```
int length = image.width * image.height * image.n;
int red[256] = {0};
int blue[256] = {0};
int green[256] = {0};

.
for(int i=0; i < length; i += image.n) {
    red[image.pixels[i]]++;
    blue[image.pixels[i+1]]++;
    green[image.pixels[i+2]]++;
}
```

In the programming example, we also calculate grayscale histogram for an image using this formula from Chaps. 1 and 3.

$$Y = 0.3R + 0.6G + 0.1G$$

© The Author(s), under exclusive licence to Springer Nature Switzerland AG 2018
B. Furht et al., *Digital Image Processing: Practical Approach*, SpringerBriefs in Computer Science, https://doi.org/10.1007/978-3-319-96634-2_4

25	32	29	29	36	34	36	27	33	26
28	35	28	36	26	38	26	38	34	31
35	25	26	32	38	29	35	26	36	29
28	32	34	25	32	27	38	30	33	26
26	35	29	27	25	32	35	29	35	37
34	28	32	36	31	29	37	35	25	29

Fig. 4.1 An example of an image 10 × 6 pixels. All values are between 0 and 255

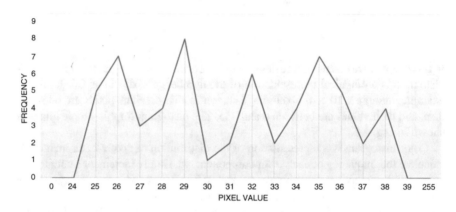

Fig. 4.2 Histogram function for a simple 10 × 6 pixels image

4.1   Program for Creating Histograms

In the demo program we wrote for this chapter, we perform the same calculation shown above. When the program is opened, it displays a single button. Clicking the button pops up a list of the files of the current working directory. When an image file is selected, the program loads the image and computes the values of the histogram for R, G, and B channels along with the grayscale values of each pixels. Figure 4.3 shows a screenshot of the demo program.

The x-axis of each plot is in the range of value between 0 and 255 as discussed already. The y-axis is the number of occurrences of each of these values. As can be observed, we have four histograms, one for each channel and one for the grayscale version of the image. ImGui does not display the values of the x and y axes initially, but hovering your mouse over the graph reveals the values in the form of a pop up. Here's a section of the code where the image is loaded and the histograms are computed:

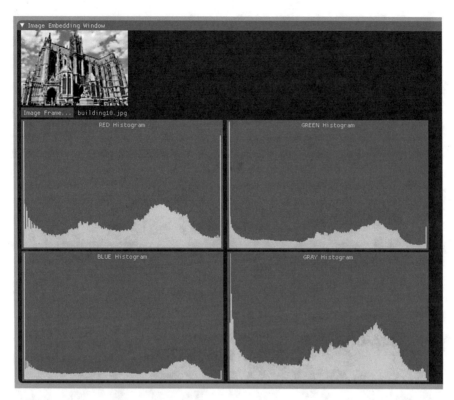

Fig. 4.3 Screenshot of the histogram program

```cpp
//opens the file list and assigns to tmp
std::string tmp = image_select(0);
if (tmp != "") {

    reset_image(&a);
    a.pixels = stbi_load(tmp.c_str(), &a.width, &a.height, &a.n, RGBA);
    assert(a.pixels != NULL);
    texture_image(&a);

    // reset arrays
    memset(red, 0, sizeof(float) * 256);
    memset(green, 0, sizeof(float) * 256);
    memset(blue, 0, sizeof(float) * 256);
    memset(gray, 0, sizeof(float) * 256);

    int length = a.width * a.height * RGBA;

    for(int i = 0; i < length; i+= RGBA) {

        red[a.pixels[i]]   +=  1.0f;
        green[a.pixels[i+1]] += 1.0f;
        blue[a.pixels[i+2]] += 1.0f;

        int grayscale = roundf((a.pixels[i] * r_gray) + (a.pixels[i+1] * g_gray) +
            (a.pixels[i+2] * b_gray));

        gray[grayscale] += + 1.0f;
    }
}
```

Once a file is selected on the pop up file list and the image is loaded, the image is given a texture. Next, we iterate through the pixels and count the frequencies of each channel. To do this, we set up four arrays at the beginning of the program before the while loop: red[256], green[256], blue[256], and gray[256]. The array size is set to 256 to account for the 0–255 component value ranges and is reset every time a new image is loaded by the memset function. Then in the inner for loop we iterate through every pixel. We access each array with the current component value and increment by one. For the red array, we use pixel pointer at index i to access the red color component. For the green array, index i + 1 of the pointer gives us the green component and finally index i + 2 gives use the blue component of each pixel. The grayscale value is acquired by implementing the equation mentioned earlier in the chapter, and the grayscale counter array is incremented with every grayscale value.

```
max_red = 0.0f;
max_green = 0.0f;
max_blue = 0.0f;
max_gray = 0.0f;

// compute max
for(int i=0; i < 256; i++) {
  max_red = MAX(red[i], max_red);
  max_green = MAX(green[i], max_green);
  max_blue = MAX(blue[i], max_blue);
  max_gray = MAX(gray[i], max_gray);
}
}

// histogram
if (a.texture_loaded) {
  ImGui::PlotHistogram("", red, 256, 0, "RED Histogram", 0.0f, max_red, ImVec2(400, 250));

  ImGui::SameLine();

  ImGui::PlotHistogram("", green, 256, 0,"GREEN Histogram", 0.0f, max_green,
ImVec2(400,250));

  ImGui::PlotHistogram("", blue, 256, 0, "BLUE Histogram", 0.0f, max_blue, ImVec2(400,250));

  ImGui::SameLine();

  ImGui::PlotHistogram("", gray, 256, 0, "GRAY Histogram", 0.0f, max_gray, ImVec2(400,250));
}
```

To display the histogram on the UI, we begin by finding the maximum value in each individual array. This is used by **ImGui** to scale the plot accordingly. Once the maximum values have been found for each array, we begin make the necessary UI calls for the histograms. ImGui library provides a simple interface with the PlotHistogram function.

After each histogram function call, ImGui::SameLine() is used as a formatting function by formatting the following histogram to be displayed on the same line as the previous histogram. If the same line function is not called after a UI function call, then by default the following UI element is displayed on a new line. For example, after the green histogram is displayed, there is no same line command, thus the blue histogram is displayed on a new line in the UI. This can be visually seen in Fig. 4.3 which captures an example of the UI in action.

In summary, we have discussed how create a histogram of pixel values of an images, store it in an array and display on the UI. We've also shown again concepts such as loading images, accessing the pixels, and displaying the image on the UI.

Chapter 5
Detecting Changes in Color

In image processing, detecting change in color between pixels is necessary for tasks like image compression and object recognition. For this chapter, we have a written a program that shows how to compute differences in RGB values of a pixel and its right and bottom neighbors. If the difference is significant, the main pixel is colored red to distinguish it from the pixels surrounding it. Coloring a pixel red is simply making its R component full value of 255, and the other components (G and B) zero.

Determining if two pixels are different can be done in two ways. The first one simply calculates the difference between each respective color components values as defined by the following formula:

$$|p1_R - p2_R| + |p1_G - p2_G| + |p1_B - p2_B|$$

where p1 and p2 are pixels and R, G, and B are the respective component values. If the sum of each difference in component values is past a certain threshold, then the main pixel is deemed to be different so it is colored red. The threshold can be any number between 0 and 765 where 765 is the maximum difference that can be achieved in the case that p1's color components are zero and p2's are all 255.

Another way to determine whether two pixels are different is done using color codes. The color code of a pixel is generated by the taking n most-significant bits of each color component byte, shifting each one with an appropriate amount, and OR-ing them together. For example, assume that a pixel has RGB values 157, 255, and 0, which are, in binary, 10011101, 11111111, and 10000000, respectively. If n is 3, the first 3 bits of each components are 100, 111, and 100. The color code then, by shifting and OR-ing the first n bits together, is 100111100. To determine if this pixel is different from its neighbors, we compare the colors codes of its neighbors with this pixel's color code, and if the codes are different, the pixel is colored red. Using more bits creates larger color codes so the pixels have a higher probability of being different.

In the demo program shown in Fig. 5.1 provides two sliders that let the user control the threshold values for the two ways of computing differences as discussed

Fig. 5.1 The program detects color changes, which are indicated in red. The program features two sliders that allows the user to switch different ways of computing differences by changing the threshold values. A threshold of 163 was applied to the image

above. The first slider, with a range of (1, 765), controls the threshold for the difference calculated with the components values. The seconds slider controls the number of bits (n) used in generating color codes for the pixels. Moving a different slider than used previously switches the way of computing differences between the pixels.

First we discuss the UI code, then the code for the difference detection of the pixels.

```
while (!glfwWindowShouldClose(window)) {

    glfwPollEvents();
    ImGui_ImplGlfwGL3_NewFrame();
    ImGui::Begin("Slider Window");

    // Select image
    if (a.texture_loaded) {
        ImGui::Image((void*)original.texture, resize_ui(a.width, a.height));
        ImGui::SameLine();
        ImGui::Image((void*)a.texture, resize_ui(a.width, a.height));

        // slider for normal threshold
        ImGui::SameLine();
        prev_thres = thres;
        ImGui::PushID("set1");
        ImGui::VSliderInt("##int", ImVec2(20,160), &thres, 1, 765);
        ImGui::PopID();

        // slider for color code difference
        ImGui::SameLine();
        prev_bits = bits;
        ImGui::PushID("set2");
```

```
        ImGui::VSliderInt("##int", ImVec2(20,160), &bits, 1, 8);
        ImGui::PopID();
    }

    if (ImGui::Button("Select Image ..."))
        ImGui::OpenPopup("select 0");
    std::string fname = image_select(0);
    ImGui::SameLine();
    if (ImGui::Button("Save Image"))
        stbi_write_png("save.png", a.width, a.height, RGBA, a.pixels, 0);

    // Image Selected, run the differences
    if (fname != "") {
        reset_image(&a);
        reset_image(&original);
        a.pixels = stbi_load(fname.c_str(), &a.width, &a.height, &a.n, RGBA);
        assert(a.pixels != NULL);
        original = a;
        original.pixels = (uint8*)malloc(a.width * a.height * RGBA);
        memcpy(original.pixels, a.pixels, a.width * a.height * RGBA);
        highlight_different(a, thres, 0);
        texture_image(&a);
        texture_image(&original);
    }

    if (prev_thres != thres) {
        memcpy(a.pixels, original.pixels, a.width * a.height * RGBA);
        reset_texture(&a);
        highlight_different(a, thres, 0);
        texture_image(&a);
    }

    if (prev_bits != bits) {
        memcpy(a.pixels, original.pixels, a.width * a.height * RGBA);
        reset_texture(&a);
        highlight_different(a, 0, bits);
        texture_image(&a);
    }
    ImGui::End();
}
```

We have already seen how to load an image from a file name that the user clicks on the file list pop up. In the if statement where an image is loaded, the image is copied to a new struct to keep a copy of the original image before we manipulate the pixel values by turning different pixels red. Next, highlight_different function is called with the loaded image, thres (threshold) value of 1, and 0 for n bits is passed as parameters. Both ways of detecting differences are handled under the same function. When 0 is passed for the thres parameter, it assumed that the third parameter n is to be used, and vice versa. Once the function returns, two textures are assigned to the original and manipulated images and are displayed by the body of the first if

statement in the while loop that checks if textures have been loaded. The two sliders
are also displayed by the same if statement with these ImGui functions:

```
ImGui::VSliderInt("##int", ImVec2(20,160), &thres, 1, 765);
// ...
ImGui::VSliderInt("##int", ImVec2(20,160), &bits, 1, 8);
```

The slider function accepts 5 parameters the first of which is the data type of the
slider. The second parameter is an ImGui vector that defines the dimension of the
slider in pixels. The third parameter is the address of the int variable that stores the
current slider value and the last two parameters is the range of the slider.

When any of the two sliders are moved the image needs to be reset to the original,
the highlight_different needs to run with the new slider value, and a new texture has
to be assigned to the image so that the result of the change in the slider can be
displayed. This is handled by the last two if statements in the while loop. The first if
statement checks if first slider has been moved by comparing the previous slider
value with the current value. The last if statement handles the change in the second
slider which controls detection with n bits.

```
// if thres is greater than zero, use RGB value to check difference
// else use color coding with n bits
void highlight_different(Image img, int thres, int n)
{
    int len = img.width * img.height * 4;

    for(int y=0; y < img.height-1; y++) {

        uint8* row  = img.pixels + (y * img.width * RGBA);
        uint8* row_next = img.pixels + ((y+1) * img.width * RGBA);

        for(int x=0; x < img.width-1; x++) {

            uint8* pixel       = row + (x * RGBA);
            uint8* pixel_right = pixel + RGBA;
            uint8* pixel_below = row_next + (x * RGBA);

            if (thres != 0) {

                int diff_right = 0;
                int diff_below = 0;

                for(int i=0; i < 3; i++) {
                    diff_right += abs(pixel[i] - pixel_right[i]);
                    diff_below += abs(pixel[i] - pixel_below[i]);
                }
```

```
                    if (diff_right > thres || diff_below > thres) {
                        pixel[0] = 255;
                        pixel[1] = 0;
                        pixel[2] = 0;
                    }
                }
                else {
                    // current pixel color code
                    int cp = (BIT_RANGE(pixel[0], 8, n) << (n * 2)) |
                            (BIT_RANGE(pixel[1], 8, n) << n) |
                            (BIT_RANGE(pixel[2], 8, n));

                    // // right code
                    int rp = (BIT_RANGE(pixel_right[0], 8, n) << (n * 2)) |
                            (BIT_RANGE(pixel_right[1], 8, n) << n) |
                            (BIT_RANGE(pixel_right[2], 8, n));

                    // // pixel below code
                    int ub = (BIT_RANGE(pixel_below[0], 8, n) << (n * 2)) |
                            (BIT_RANGE(pixel_below[1], 8, n) << n) |
                            (BIT_RANGE(pixel_below[2], 8, n));

                    if (cp != rp || cp != ub) {
                        pixel[0] = 255;
                        pixel[1] = 0;
                        pixel[2] = 0;
                    }
                }
            }
        }
    }
}
```

In highlight_different function, there are two nested loops that iterate through every row and every column of each row in the image. However, the pixels of the image are not organized in rows and columns in memory. The pointer that is returned from the stbi_load function points to the address memory of the first component of the first pixel in the image and rest of the pixels follow along in sequential order. As a result, we need to do some pointer arithmetic to move the pointer around to the pixel we want to access. As can be seen in Fig. 5.2, in a 2×2 image, we need to add 6 bytes to the pointer to go from the first pixel of the first row to the first pixel of the second row. The first pixel of the second row is directly above the first pixel in the image so in general to access the pixel directly below a pixel, we need to add the number of bytes in width of the image to the pointer.

```
uint8* row =  img.pixels + (y * img.width * RGBA);
uint8* row_next = img.pixels + ((y+1) * img.width * RGBA);
```

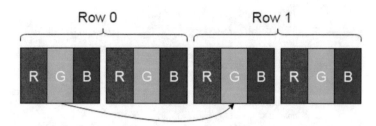

Fig. 5.2 A 2 × 2 image in memory. To go from the first pixel of row 1 to the first pixel of row two, width × 3 (RGB) bytes needs to be added to the pointer pointing to the first pixel in the image

In the function, to calculate the pointer address of each row, we run the first line in the code sample above. For example, if we are currently on row two, then (2 * img. width * RGBA) results in the amount of bytes we need to add to the base pointer to acquire the address of the start of the second row. To access the next row, it requires the same computation but with y incremented once. We only need to add the number of bytes in one pixel to access the pixel directly to the right which you can observe in the code sample below:

```
uint8* pixel       = row + (x * RGBA);
uint8* pixel_right = pixel + RGBA;
uint8* pixel_below = row_next + (x * RGBA);
```

Once we have access the current pixel, pixel to the right, and the pixel below, we can check if the current pixel is different using one of the two ways. Using the component value and a threshold value, detecting difference is done as such:

```
for(int i=0; i < 3; i++) {
    diff_right += abs(pixel[i] - pixel_right[i]);
    diff_below += abs(pixel[i] - pixel_below[i]);
}

// color red if either neighbor pixel is past the threshold
if (diff_right > sens || diff_below > sens) {
    pixel[0] = 255;
    pixel[1] = 0;
    pixel[2] = 0;
}
```

If the difference is to be detected using color codes, then the color code of a pixel is computed as such:

```
int color_code = (BIT_RANGE(pixel[0], 8, n) << (n * 2)) |
                 (BIT_RANGE(pixel[1], 8, n) << n) |
                 (BIT_RANGE(pixel[2], 8, n));
```

BIT_RANGE is a macro that returns n bits to right of the bit position provided by the second parameter shifted to right to replace the n least significant bits. To see this in action, let's work with an example where the components are 10011101 (R), 11111111 (G), and 10000000 (B) and n is three. BIT_RANGE(R, 8, 3) results in 00000100 where the bits from the 8th bit to the 6th bit are moved all way to the right. In the code sample these bits of R get shifted the left n x 2 times. This is because we want the n most significant bits of each component to be aligned in order in one number. So, 00000100 shifted 6 times to the left becomes 100000000. The green component goes through the same process but the final value gets shifted 3 times, and the green component does not get the final left shift at all. The final values are as following:

100000000 – R
000111000 – G
000000100 – B

To combine everything under one 9 bit number we simply OR everything together and arrive at 1001111000 which is the 3 bit color code of the pixel. After computing the color codes of the neighbor pixels, if any of the codes are different, then the pixel is deemed different and is colored red.

In this chapter, we discussed the layout of multi-row images in memory and how we can access neighboring pixels to detect change in pixel values. We showed two ways of detecting difference, which involved bit manipulation and introduced new UI components of the ImGui library.

Chapter 6
Lossless JPEG Image Compression

The main reasons for compression in multimedia systems are: (1) large storage requirements of multimedia data, (2) relatively slow storage devices which do not allow playing back uncompressed multimedia data in real time, and (3) the network bandwidth which does not allow real-time video data transmission.

In this section we focus on image compression, which can be classified into two major groups: lossless and lossy image compression. As the names may infer, with lossless compression, the data that is compressed and the data acquired after decompression are exactly the same. Lossy compression however makes no guarantees about the exactness of the compressed and decompressed data. Lossy compression techniques usually score higher compression ratios since it can leverage the lossy nature of the compression to reduce file size.

The JPEG standard for image compression is targeted for full color images, JPEG standard provides four modes of operations, three modes are for lossy compression, and one is for lossless compression. We describe and implement in this chapter the lossless JPEG image compression, which is still applicable in some critical applications, where the original image is fully recovered and reproduced. These applications include various medical applications and space exploration applications.

Image codec consists of image encoder that compresses an image, and image decoder that decompresses an image. JPEG lossless encoder is shown in Fig. 6.1.

The encoder consists of two major components: (a) predictor, and (b) entropy encoder, typically Huffman encoder. Predictor block diagram, shown in Fig. 6.2, calculates the difference between the current pixel (or sample) X from neighboring samples (A, B, and C).

The JPEG standard defines seven possible predictors, which define the prediction x as a function of A, B, and C. These seven predictors are shown in Table 6.1.

The second block in the JPEG lossless encoder is entropy encoder, which is based of Huffman encoder, as shown in Fig. 6.3.

© The Author(s), under exclusive licence to Springer Nature Switzerland AG 2018   35
B. Furht et al., *Digital Image Processing: Practical Approach*, SpringerBriefs in
Computer Science, https://doi.org/10.1007/978-3-319-96634-2_6

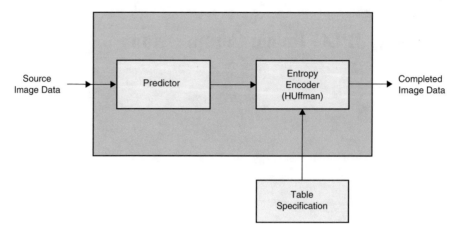

Fig. 6.1 JPEG lossless encoder

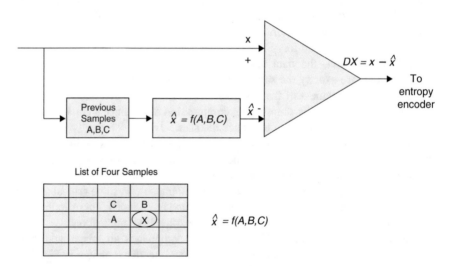

Fig. 6.2 The block diagram of the predictor in lossless JPEG encoder

Huffman is a statistical encoding algorithm, which defines high probably symbols with short codes and less probably symbols with larger codes. It is one of the simplest but effective lossless data compression algorithms.

Table 6.1 Predictors in JPEG lossless encoding

Selection value	Predictor value
0	No prediction
1	$\hat{x} = A$
2	$\hat{x} = B$
3	$\hat{x} = C$
4	$\hat{x} = A + B - C$
5	$x = A + \frac{B-C}{2}$
6	$x = B + \frac{A-C}{2}$
7	$x = \frac{A+B}{2}$

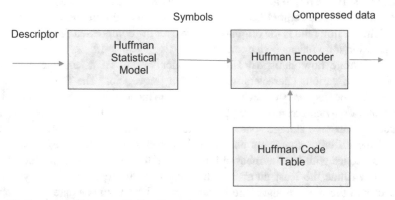

Fig. 6.3 Entropy coding using Huffman encoder

6.1 Example of a Huffman coder

To go along with this section on Huffman coding, we have written a command-line program that can compresses any file using strictly Huffman coding. To compress a file, simply run this command:

```
huff test.txt
```

The command will output a new file called test.txt.huff which will be the compressed file. To decompress and extract the original content, run this command:

```
huff -d test.txt.huff -o decompressed_test.txt
```

The decompressed data will be written to the output file decompressed_test.txt as defined in our command. You can use this tool to compress any file you want. The more redundant the data in your file, the higher the compression ratios will be. In our test runs, an 887 KB file containing only the character 'A' compressed down to only

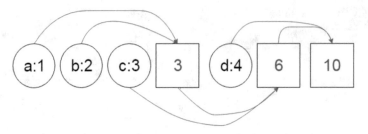

Fig. 6.4 Circle nodes are character frequencies and square nodes are the sum nodes

4 KB bytes! However, in reality, entropy may be a lot higher. A 74 KB book written by Charles Dickens compressed down to 44 Kb with a compression ratio of almost 1.7. Compression ratio is the original file size over the compressed file size. A higher compression ratio means better compression.

To illustrate how statistical Huffman coder works, let us assume a text file consisting of various characters with different frequencies. The first step consists of counting the frequency of each character/byte in the text file. By identifying which characters or bytes are more frequent, fewer bits can be used to represent these characters and save storage space. With Huffman coding, we first scan the file to record the different characters and their frequencies in the file. Next, we assign Huffman codes with least number of bits required to the most frequent characters.

To determine the least number of bits and code to be used for every unique character in the file, the algorithm builds a tree where the nodes are the character frequencies and special nodes that are the sum of each character frequency. Here is a simple example that illustrates this process. The following is data sequence that we intend to compress: 'abbcccdddd'. The algorithm first counts the frequencies of the characters and sort the numbers in ascending order. We treat every frequency number as a node in a tree. Then going from left to right, every pair of number is summed together and the result is inserted back into the list in sorted fashion, as illustrated in Fig. 6.4.

The new sum node also becomes the parent of the two frequencies added together node in the Huffman tree, as shown in Fig. 6.5.

Once the tree is completed, every left branch is assigned '0' and right branches value '1'. The trail of zeros and ones from the root node (top of the tree) to the leaf (character nodes) are the Huffman codes for every character. Regardless of how deep the tree may get, Huffman codes will never repeat, so code collision for different byte values is not an issue. Notice that in our data 'd' is the most frequent. Thus, our Huffman tree assigned a single bit '1' to this character. On the other hand, 'a', being the least frequent character, is assigned the Huffman code '000' for a total of 3 bits. Putting everything together, our new compressed data using Huffman code is as follows:

```
000 001 001 01 01 01 1 1 1 1
 a   b   b   c  c  c  d d d d
```

Fig. 6.5 As nodes pairs are
summed, the tree is built
bottom up

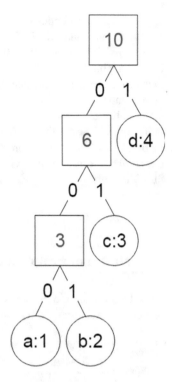

Now that we can represent characters with values than a byte, we need pack this
stream of bits into 8-bit bytes values which looks as such:

```
00000100 10101011 11100000
 a   b    b c c c d ddd
```

After the last '1', we fill the rest of the byte with zeros. The total number of bits
required to represent the data is now only 19 bits or 3 bytes whereas before, for
10 characters, 80 bits (8 bits per byte) was needed which gives us a compression ratio
of 3.33 (10 bytes/3 bytes).

Our work isn't finished yet. If the new compressed data is stored in a new file,
without also recording the Huffman tree in some way which lets us know what every
bit might represent, decompressing the file is not possible. Thus, at the start of every
compressed file, a Huffman table that contains the Huffman code and bit count for
each byte value must be recorded. With the table added, our compressed file may
look as such:

```
3 a 3 0 b 3 1 c 2 1 d 1 1
10 00000100 10101011 11100000
```

The first line contains the table which includes byte value, bit count of the Huffman code, and the Huffman code as a number value for every unique byte in the original data, respectively. The first number is the number of the characters in the Huffman table which in this case is 3. The first byte of the second line indicates how many total characters was compressed, and the rest of the file is the bits we acquired after compression. Since only 3 bytes is required for every unique character in the table, in this case, the size of the table is 12 bytes. Table length and total characters indicators add two bytes. With 3 bytes from the compressed data, our new file size is 17 bytes, resulting in a compression ratio of 0.59 (10/17). The Huffman table tanked the compression ratio but, without it, the file cannot be decompressed. For larger files, the Huffman table may not impact the ratio as much as it did with our trivial example.

6.2 Huffman Programming Example

Let's begin with the compression step in main.cpp. Once the file we want to compress is acquired, with a single function, we are able to compress the file.

```
int str_len;
// acquire file content and length
uint8* str = (uint8*)fget(fname, &str_len);

std::vector<uint8> cfile = huffman_compress(str, str_len); // compress
```

The compression step begins with counting byte frequencies. Next, the frequencies get sorted in ascending order and only the byte values with frequencies greater than zero are selected. Knowing the frequencies, we build the Huffman tree and compress the entire file, byte at a time, with the codes acquired from the tree. The compression function is shown below:

```
struct huff_node {
    huff_node* left = nullptr;
    huff_node* right = nullptr;
    unsigned int code = 0;
    int bit_count = 0;
    int freq = 0;
    int value = 0; // 0 - 255 for byte, -1 for sum node
};

std::vector<uint8> huffman_compress(uint8* str, int str_len)
{
    // count frequency of each byte in the data
    std::vector<huff_node> hn = byte_frequency(str, str_len);

    // only keep bytes whose frequency is greater than zero
    auto nonzero_iterator = std::find_if(hn.begin(), hn.end(), [](const huff_node& a)
        -> bool {return a.freq != 0;});

    hn = std::vector<huff_node> (nonzero_iterator, hn.end());
    build_huffman_tree(hn);
    std::vector<uint8> cfile = huffman_cmpres(str, str_len, hn);
    return cfile;
}
```

Let's discuss the building of tree. As explained above, before we create the tree, we need to add the pair of frequencies and insert the total back into the list while making sure the list remains sorted. There is a C++ standard library container that can do just that. With priority queue, as we push new numbers into the list, the container will automatically keep the list sorted. As we add new pairs together, we also establish necessary connections of the nodes to build up our tree. Trees can be built with left and right pointers from the parent node to the children nodes and that is exactly what we do. We assign -1 to the sum node to distinguish it from regular frequency nodes. Here is the code for the tree creation:

```cpp
void build_huffman_tree(std::vector<huff_node>& hn)
{
    // ascending priority_queue
    std::priority_queue<huff_node*, std::vector<huff_node*>, nodes_comp> nodes;

    // push the memory of the huffman nodes
    for (int i=0; i < hn.size(); i++)
        nodes.push((huff_node*)&hn[i]);

    // create node connections
    while(nodes.size() > 1) {
        huff_node* a = nodes.top();
        nodes.pop();
        huff_node* b = nodes.top();
        nodes.pop();

        huff_node* sum_node = new huff_node;
        sum_node->value = -1; // sum node indicator
        sum_node->freq = a->freq + b->freq;
        sum_node->left = a;
        sum_node->right = b;
        nodes.push(sum_node);
    }

    huff_node* root = nodes.top();
    assign_code(root, 0, 0);
}

void assign_code(huff_node* node, int code, int bit_count) {

    if(node == nullptr)
        return;

    // not sum node
    if(node->value != -1) {
        node->code = code;
        node->bit_count = bit_count;
    }

    // code must not exceed 16 bits, since our table only allows 2 byte codes
    if (bit_count > 24) {
        std::cout << "ERROR: huffman tree has exceeded depth 16";
        exit(1);
    }

    int left_code = (code << 1); // shift left
    int right_code = (code << 1) | 1; // shift left and OR 1

    //traverse the tree and assign left branches code + 0, and right branches code + 1
    assign_code(node->left, left_code, bit_count+1);
    assign_code(node->right, right_code, bit_count+1);
}
```

Table 6.2 HUFF file layout

4 bytes	1 byte	~	4 bytes	~
HUFF	Table size	Huffman table	Original file size	Compressed data

Once the tree is created, starting with the root node, we traverse through the entire tree recursively and assign "0" to the left child branch and "1" to the right child branch. The code and bit count originally starts with zeros. To create a new code for the left branch, a "0" gets inserted into the number by bit shifting the previous code to the left once. To clarify how this works, let's work with an example. The previous code assigned to the parent node above is, say, "0101" in binary. Shifting the number left once results in "01010". It simply moves every bit once to the left and inserts a new zero at the beginning which is exactly what we need. For the right branch, inserting a "1" requires the same operation but this time we need to OR the shifted value with "1" to turn the newly inserted bit to 1 which results in "01011".

The next step is to finally compress the data and create our HUFF file. The layout of any HUFF is defined in Table 6.2. The first four bytes is the file signature defined by the string 'HUFF'. This is not necessary at all but it's a nice touch. In the next byte, we store the table size of the Huffman table. This is required because the Huffman table can contain any number of Huffman codes from 0 to 255 unique codes. The table allocates for each character 1 byte for the original character value, 1 byte for bit count, and 3 bytes for the Huffman code. The next 4 bytes tells us the original size of the file in bytes and the rest of the file contains the compressed data. You can observe all of this in the Huffman_cmpres function.

```
// top part of huffman_cmpres function

std::vector<uint8> cstr; //compressed string
cstr.reserve(str_len);

//signature
cstr.push_back('H');
cstr.push_back('U');
cstr.push_back('F');
cstr.push_back('F');

//table size
cstr.push_back(hn.size()); // if size == 256, then 0 is recorded

// table , 2 bytes for code, 1 byte for bit_count, and 1 byte for byte value
for(int j=0; j < hn.size(); j++) {
    cstr.push_back(hn[j].code >> 16);
    cstr.push_back(hn[j].code >> 8);
    cstr.push_back(hn[j].code);
    cstr.push_back(hn[j].bit_count);
    cstr.push_back(hn[j].value);
}

//record file size, 4 bytes
cstr.push_back(str_len >> 24);
cstr.push_back(str_len >> 16);
cstr.push_back(str_len >> 8);
cstr.push_back(str_len);
```

Table 6.3 An example of a HUFF header

Signature, 1 byte	Table Size, 1 byte	Table, 20 bytes <character>< bit count><code>	File Size, 4 bytes
HUFF	4	a 3 0 b 3 1 c 2 1 d 1 1	10

In the program, "cstr" is a vector that contains the content of the HUFF file. You can observe above how the header of any HUFF file is created. To record the original file size, notice that we use shifting again. Since the str_len variable is an int, it has 4 bytes and we need to shift to the right by increments of 8 bits to record every byte, starting with the most significant one. If the file size in binary is "00100001 00110010 10100011 11010000", we shift the entire 32 bit number to the right 24 positions, discarding all the bytes to the right. The resultant byte is 0010000 which gets pushed into the vector. Next, we shift by 16 which results in 00100001 00110010 but since the vector has type uint8, only the first, least significant byte, is recorded. Next, we shift by 8 times, and record the third byte, and finally the fourth byte by not shifting at all. We have thus recorded all four bytes of the size variable. Table 6.3 contains the HUFF header for the sequence 'abbcccdddd'.

With the table established, the next step is to iterate over every character, look up its Huffman code, and pack the bits of the code inside 8-bit bytes. Packing is necessary because the smallest unit of data is the 8-bit byte and if we were to write the Huffman code to our file vector as is without packing, a code that is potentially smaller than 8 bits would get converted in an 8-bit byte (uint8) before being written to the vector, which defeats the purpose of compression. As a result, we need to pack multiple codes into one byte before writing.

To pack a stream of bits, we start with the most significant bit of the byte being written to and record every bit of the code from left to right. Every 8 bits, we write the full byte to the vector and resume writing to a new byte. For the sequence 'abbcccdddd', packing is shown in Table 6.4.

The code for the packing process is shown below:

```
// packing codes into bytes and storing the bytes in the vector
    for(int j=0; j < str_len; j++) {

        dictionary d = dict[*str++];
        int bit_count = d.bit_count;
        int code = d.code;

        // current byte has enough available bits for code
        if (bit_pos > bit_count) {
            bit_pos -= bit_count;       •
            b |= code << bit_pos;
        }
        else {
            bit_count -= bit_pos;
            b |= code >> bit_count;
            cstr.push_back(b);
            while (bit_count >= 8) { // loop for codes with large amount of bits
                bit_count -= 8;
                cstr.push_back(code >> bit_count);
            }
            b = code << (8 - bit_count);
            bit_pos = 8 - bit_count;
        }
```

Table 6.4 The bits of the Huffman code are packed together inside bytes

	Byte 1	Byte 2	Byte 3
Bit	1 2 3 4 5 6 7 8	1 2 3 4 5 6 7 8	1 2 3 4 5 6 7 8
a	0 0 0		
b	0 0 1		
b	0 0	1	
c		0 1	
c		0 1	
c		0 1	
d		1	
d			1
d			1
d			1

```
        // check if end of byte is reached, if yes, write then reset
        if (bit_pos == 0) {
            cstr.push_back(b);
            bit_pos = 8;
            b = 0;
        }
    }

    if (bit_pos != 8) {
        cstr.push_back(b);
    }
```

The loop is broken into two parts. The first "if" statement checks to see if the current byte being written to has enough bits to store the current code and if so, the code bits is written into the byte starting from the current bit position of the byte. The second handles cases where the code has more bits than the byte has room so as many bits from the code as the current byte allows is written, then the byte is stored in the vector and then reset to zero with the bit position set to the 8th bit. Next, the leftover bits from the code are written to the start of the byte. Both of these cases can be seen in action in Table 6.4.

In our huff program, to decompress any file, we run the huffman_decompress function. Here is the function in its entirety:

```cpp
std::vector<uint8> huffman_decompress(uint8* str, int len)
{
    int i = 0;

    std::string magic((char*)str, 4); // first 4 characters must be HUFF
    if (magic != "HUFF") {
        std::cout << "ERROR: file is not a HUFF file";
        exit(1);
    }
    i+=4;

    // getting table
    int table_size = str[i++];
    if (table_size == 0)
        table_size = 256;

    dictionary dict[table_size];
    for(int j=0; j < table_size; j++) {
        int code = (str[i] << 16) | (str[i+1] << 8) | str[i+2];
        i += 3;
        dict[j].code = code;
        dict[j].bit_count = str[i++];
        dict[j].value = str[i++];
    }

    int decompressed_len = (str[i] << 24) | (str[i+1] << 16) | (str[i+2] << 8) | str[i+3];
    i+=4;

    // get fewest_bits
    int fewest_bits = dict[table_size-1].bit_count;

    // get 8 bytes total-bits
    std::vector<uint8> dstr; //decompressed file
    dstr.reserve(len * 2); // reserve some memory, not exact
    int bit_pos = 8;
    int b = str[i++];
    int val;

    for(int j=0; j < decompressed_len; j++) {

        int c = 0, next = 0;
        int cbc = fewest_bits; // CurrentBitCount

        do {
            if (bit_pos >= cbc)
                c = b >> (bit_pos - cbc);
```

```
else {
    b = (b << 8) | str[i++];
    bit_pos += 8;
    c = b >> (bit_pos - cbc);
}

// search dict for code and bit_count match
for (int j=0; j < table_size; j++) {
    if (dict[j].bit_count == cbc && dict[j].code == c) {
        val = dict[j].value;
        next = 1;
    }
}
```

Decompression of a HUFF file involves reading the table size, the table, and the original file size bytes before decompressing the compressed data as we do in the first part of the function. Since the compressed data is a sequence of Huffman codes, the body of the loop unpacks bits from the current byte and matches it with the codes in the Huffman table. If the current bit count of the unpacked code and the code itself matches an entry in the table, the character value gets stored in the vector. The loop repeats until all the original characters are unpacked from the compressed data.

Huffman coding is a general compression algorithm and the huff program can compress any file or sequence of data. We present next lossless JPEG compression examples and how we can decrease the entropy of the data to improve the ratio of Huffman compression.

6.3   Lossless JPEG Examples

To illustrate how the lossless JPEG encoder works, we show two examples, one for the prediction $x = A$ (Fig. 6.6), and the second example for the predictor $x = A + B - C$ (Fig. 6.7).

In both examples the image is a very small, 4×2 pixels, and the encoding process consists of two steps (1) Predictor and (2) Huffman encoder, as illustrated in Fig. 6.1. In the first step the pixel differences are calculated using two different predictors. The first pixel (72) remains the same. In the second step, the Huffman table (Table 6.5) was used to convert the pixel differences to Huffman codes. Again, the first pixel (72) was binary encoded as eight-bit number '01001100'.

Let's calculate the obtained compression ratio in the two examples. The number of bits in the original 4×2 image was 8 pixels $\times$ 8 bits $= 64$ bits. In the first example the compressed image consists of 38 bits, so the compression ratio is $64/38 = 1.68$. In the second example, the compression ratio is $64/32 = 2$, so in this example Predictor 4 gave better results than Predictor 1.

Note that for any selected predictor (1–7), the first row should always use the predictor $x = A$, because there are no other two neighboring pixels B and C. Similarly, the predictor for the first column must be always $x = B$, because there are no two other neighboring pixels A and C. This is illustrated in Fig. 6.8.

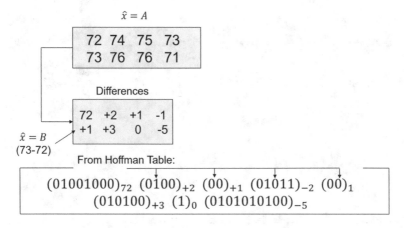

Fig. 6.6 Lossless JPEG example 1: x = A

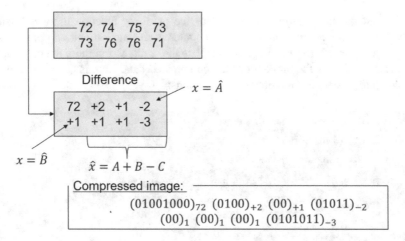

Fig. 6.7 Lossless JPEG example 2: x = A + B − C

Table 6.5 Huffman table for differences

Difference DX	Code
0	1
1	00
−1	011
2	0100
−2	01011
3	010100
−3	0101011
4	01010100
−4	010101011
5	0101010100
−5	01010101011
6	010101010100
−6	0101010101011

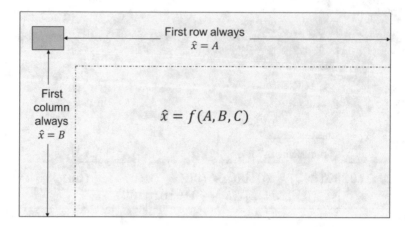

Fig. 6.8 Lossless JPEG selection of predictors

To test out the compression ratios for the predictor function used in lossless JPEG, we wrote a small program. It computes each function and compresses the results using Huffman encoding. To calculate the compression ratio, the original bit count is divided by the bit count of the compressed data. Here is the section of the program that computes the prediction functions:

```
uint8* pixels = stbi_load(filename, &width, &height, &n, 0);
int j=0;
for(int y=0; y < height; y++) {

    uint8* X = pixels + (y * width * n);

    for(int x=0; x < width; x++, X += n, j += 3) {

        /*
        C B
        A X
        */
        uint8* A = NULL; // left pixel
        uint8* B = NULL; // above pixel
        uint8* C = NULL; // diagonal pixel

        // seven predictions
        for(int i=0; i < 7; i++) {

            // formula do not apply to first row and column
            if (y == 0 && x > 0) {
                A = X - n;
                prediction[i][j]   = X[0] - A[0];
                prediction[i][j+1] = X[1] - A[1];
                prediction[i][j+2] = X[2] - A[2];
            }
            else if (x==0 && y > 0) {
                B = X - (width * n);
                prediction[i][j]   = X[0] - B[0];
                prediction[i][j+1] = X[1] - B[1];
                prediction[i][j+2] = X[2] - B[2];
            }

            // apply appropriate formula
            else if (y > 0 && x > 0) {

                A = X - n;
                B = X - (width * n);
                C = A - (width * n);
```

```
// prediction 1 - 7
if (i==0) {
    prediction[i][j]   = X[0] - A[0];
    prediction[i][j+1] = X[1] - A[1];
    prediction[i][j+2] = X[2] - A[2];
}
else if (i==1) {
    prediction[i][j]   = X[0] - B[0];
    prediction[i][j+1] = X[1] - B[1];
    prediction[i][j+2] = X[2] - B[2];
}
else if (i==2) {
    prediction[i][j]   = X[0] - C[0];
    prediction[i][j+1] = X[1] - C[1];
    prediction[i][j+2] = X[2] - C[2];
}
else if (i==3) {
    prediction[i][j]   = X[0] - (A[0] + B[0] - C[0]);
    prediction[i][j+1] = X[1] - (A[1] + B[1] - C[1]);
    prediction[i][j+2] = X[2] - (A[2] + B[2] - C[2]);
}
else if (i==4) {
    prediction[i][j]   = X[0] - (A[0] + (B[0] - C[0]) / 2);
    prediction[i][j+1] = X[1] - (A[1] + (B[1] - C[1]) / 2);
    prediction[i][j+2] = X[2] - (A[2] + (B[2] - C[2]) / 2);
}
else if (i==5) {
    prediction[i][j]   = X[0] - (B[0] + (A[0] - C[0]) / 2);
    prediction[i][j+1] = X[1] - (B[1] + (A[1] - C[1]) / 2);
    prediction[i][j+2] = X[2] - (B[2] + (A[2] - C[2]) / 2);
}
else if (i==6) {
    prediction[i][j]   = X[0] - ((A[0] + B[0]) / 2);
    prediction[i][j+1] = X[1] - ((A[1] + B[1]) / 2);
    prediction[i][j+2] = X[2] - ((A[2] + B[2]) / 2);
}
            }
        }
    }
}
```

Because each sample/pixel is composed of three channels R, G, and B, the predictor is computed three times for each respective color component. Also included in this code sample is pointer management to select pixels that are neighbors of the current pixel using simple pointer arithmetic. To select a pixel to the left of the current pixel, we must subtract 3 bytes from the current pointer for every byte of R, G, and B. To select the pixel directly above in the previous row, we must subtract one row worth of bytes which is the width of the image times number of channels, three in this case, from the pointer. Going diagonally up and left is the combination of the two operations.

Results for compression ratios for two color images and for seven predictors are shown in Fig. 6.9. For image 1 the best predictor was Predictor 4 achieving 1.86 compression ratio, while for image 2 Predictor 5 with compression ratio of 2.02. Notice that compressing the image as is without using a Predictor function resulted in the lowest compression ratios in both images showing that processing with some predictor lowers the entropy of the data which improves compression.

Predictor	Ratio
1	1.702152
2	1.683111
3	1.584306
4	1.863306
5	1.805943
6	1.790550
7	1.817624
No Predictor	1.041141

Predictor	Ratio
1	1.983214
2	1.651792
3	1.612396
4	1.951132
5	2.029998
6	1.840108
7	1.898065
No Predictor	1.065430

Fig. 6.9 Lossless JPEG applied to two images. Seven predictors are used

In summary, this chapter presented the practical design of lossless image compression using a predictor and Huffman statistical coder. We showed that Predictor functions generally improve compression ratio by lowering the entropy of the data. Next, we discuss image retrieval based on pixel similarity.

Chapter 7
Similarity-Based Image Retrieval

So far, we have only dealt with topics involving one or two images. The program demos were mostly about loading an image and performing a task e.g. converting to grayscale or hiding data in an image. With image retrieval, however, our task is to search for images from a large collection or database that are similar, in some manner, to a selected image. Measuring similarity can be done in many ways and depends on the problem at hand. There are techniques that involve analyzing images based on metadata e.g. file name, tags, etc. that are affiliated with the image. Other ways are based on the content of the image rather than metadata by processing the pixel values in some way. For this chapter, we've collected 200 images of various scenes and objects that make up the database which can be found in the 'db' folder in this chapter's directory. The demo program is hard coded to work with these images, but you may change that by altering the source code and recompiling.

In the demo program (Fig. 7.1), image retrieval is performed using image histograms with color codes. We've already discussed color codes in Chap. 5 where each color components' most significant n bits are combined to produce a single value. The slider next to the selected image controls the number of bits to be used for the color codes which is capped at four due to the huge amount of memory required to store all the images and histogram values in memory. We use these color code values to create a histogram for each image in the database which is then used to compute the difference (error) with the selected image. The top six images with the least amount of difference are displayed below the selected image. The histogram difference values are also displayed at the bottom of the UI. Notice that because the selected image is part of the database, the histogram difference with itself is zero and therefore it gets displayed first.

© The Author(s), under exclusive licence to Springer Nature Switzerland AG 2018
B. Furht et al., *Digital Image Processing: Practical Approach*, SpringerBriefs in
Computer Science, https://doi.org/10.1007/978-3-319-96634-2_7

Fig. 7.1 Image retrieval using color codes and histogram

```
//sets up the database and opens all the images at once
// returns a sorted vector from most similar to least similar
std::vector<histogram> db_retrieve(histogram& main_histo, int bits)
{
    // all the filenames in 'db' folder
    static std::vector<std::string> fnames = dirlist("db", FILES_ONLY);
    static std::vector<histogram> db(fnames.size());
    static int init = 0;

    main_histo.set_histogram(bits);

    // Create texture for all the images in 'db' directory once
    if (!init) {
        for(int i=0; i < db.size(); i++) {
            db[i].image.pixels = stbi_load(("db/"+fnames[i]).c_str(),
                db[i].image.width, &db[i].image.height, &db[i].image.n, RGBA);

            texture_image(&db[i].image);
        }
        init = 1;
    }

    // Get the histogram difference, and return sorted vector
    for(int i=0; i < db.size(); i++) {
        db[i].set_histogram(bits);
        db[i].difference = hist_dif(db[i].values, main_histo.values, bits);
    }

    // sort vector of histograms ascendingly based on histogram difference
    std::sort(db.begin(), db.end(), [](const histogram& a, const histogram& b) ->
        bool { return a.difference < b.difference;});

    return db;
}
```

Once an image is selected, db_retrieve function is called with a reference to the histogram of the select image and the number of bits used to create the color code. At the start of the function the names of the files in the 'db' folder are acquired with dirlist and a vector that will hold all the histogram for these image files is initialized.

Next, in the first loop, the image files are loaded and new textures are created. This part along with the initialization of the vectors at the start of the function only occur once in the lifetime of the program. When a new image is selected by the user, since the images in the database are already loaded, we can skip directly to the image retrieval part. In the second loop and right after, we create histograms for the images using set_histogram, calculate the difference between the main histogram and the image in the current iteration with hist_dif, and finally sort the vector containing the histogram differences.

```
// starting at bit s, get f bits to the right of s shifted all the way to the
right,while discarding bits outside of the range [s, s-f)
// ex: val = 1001101, bits_range(val,4,2) -> 00000011
#define BIT_RANGE(val, s, f) (((val) &= (1 << (s)) - 1) >> ((s) - (f)))
#define MAX_BITS 4
struct histogram
{
    void set_histogram(int bits)
    {
        //allocates memory for max possible number of bits for RGB
        if (!values)
            values = (int*)malloc(sizeof(int) * (1 << ( MAX_BITS * 3));

        // only set the amount of bits needed to zero, hence 1 << (bits * 3)
        //just clears the necessary amount of memory
        memset(values, 0, sizeof(int) * (1 << (bits * 3)));

        uint8* pixels = image.pixels;
        int len = image.width * image.height * RGBA;

        for(int i=0; i < len; i += RGBA) {
            int r = BIT_RANGE(pixels[ i ], 8, bits) << (bits * 2);
            int g = BIT_RANGE(pixels[i+1], 8, bits) << bits;
            int b = BIT_RANGE(pixels[i+2], 8, bits);
            values[r | g | b]++;
        }
    }

    int* values = NULL;
    int difference = 0;
    Image image;
};

// difference between the frequency of color codes between two images
int hist_dif(int* a, int* b, int bits)
{
    int len = 1 << (bits * 3);
    int dif = 0;
    for(int i=0; i < len; i++) {
        dif += abs(a[i] - b[i]);
    }
    return dif;
}
```

Each image and histogram is represented using the struct above. The values pointer contains the histogram values, difference is assigned the computed difference using the function hist_diff, and the image is the image struct we've used before.

While the smallest color code possible is zero, the maximum value depends on the number of bits of the color codes. If three bits are used per each RGB component then the maximum value is a number with 9 bits with all 1 s. Since the number of bits allowed is capped at four bits, we allocate the maximum size memory we need for each histogram in set_histogram within the first if statement by shifting a one to the left maximum number of bits positions. Memory is only allocated once hence why maximum amount of memory required needs to be allocated. Next, in this function, before the loop, the memory allocated is set to zero. In the loop, the bits are extracted from each component and combined to create a color code which is then used to as an index in the histogram values, and the number at that index is incremented once.

Calculating the difference between two histograms is done with hist_difference function. The values pointers are of the selected image and an image from the database are passed as parameters as well as the number of bits used for the color codes. In the loop, the absolute value of the difference between the two values at each index is summed. Finally, the sum is returned which is then used to sort the images by their histogram differences. Changing the number of bits by moving the slider affects the computed differences as shown in Fig. 7.2.

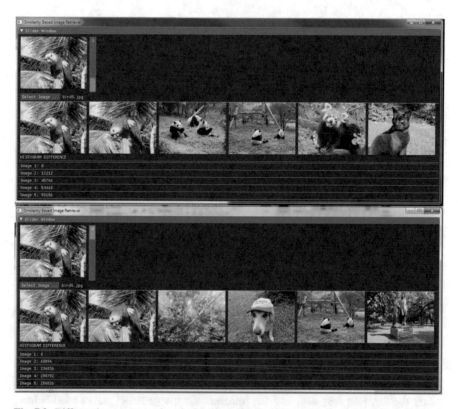

Fig. 7.2 Different images are retrieved when the number of bits used in the color codes is changed

```
//image select opens all the image list and assigns to fname
std::string fname = image_select(0);
if (fname != "") {
    reset_image(&main_histo.image);
    main_histo.image.pixels = stbi_load(fname.c_str(),
&main_histo.image.width,
        &main_histo.image.height, &main_histo.image.n, RGBA);
    assert(main_histo.image.pixels != NULL);
    texture_image(&main_histo.image);
    db_histograms = db_retrieve(main_histo, bits);
}

// Slider moved
if (bits != prev_bits)
    db_histograms = db_retrieve(main_histo, bits);
```

In the main while loop, db_retrieve is called when an image is selected or the slider is moved. The function then creates the histogram values for each image in the database and calculates the differences. The returned value is a sorted vector of the histogram structs. Next, using the textures of the first most similar six images are displayed.

We've discussed the basics of content based image retrieval using color coding and histograms. Although there are many more methods, some involving machine learning, we feel that the use of histograms, which is well within the scope and introductory nature of this book, is a viable method for this task so we will stop here. Next, we return to topics involving one or two images and explore transition animations between two images.

Chapter 8
Data Hiding in Digital Images

Steganography is the art of hiding a piece of data within a transferred message. The secret data must be concealed in a way such that anyone observing the message should not notice any artifacts of its concealment. In our case, the message is an image file and the secret piece of data is any file we wish to hide.

Data, files, and memory stored in a computer are all represented by streams of bits and bytes. Opening, manipulating, uploading, and downloading files all operate at the byte level. At the computer level, there is no higher abstraction that can represent stored data and computer commands. As we previously discussed, digital images are made up of pixels. Each pixel's color is represented by a combination of RGB color components. Each color component is one byte, or 8-bits, so the range of values in base 10 for each component is between 0 and 255. Knowing this, we can hide data within every pixel. The least significant bit of each color component can be altered in a way such that a stream of those bits can be made to have a meaningful message. The message can be anything from a simple "Hello, World" string to the content of another file. If we choose to only use the least significant bit, then to produce a single meaningful byte of information, 8 consecutive color components must be altered to contain the byte.

In Fig. 8.1, each bit in 11011011 is written to consecutive color components. To write the byte into the color components, we must start with the 8th bit in the byte and alter the first color component's least significant bit to match that of the byte. Next, we make the next color component's first bit to match the 7th bit of the byte we are writing. These steps repeat until all 8-bits override the least significant bits of 8 color components. To write the next byte, we begin with the next color component from where we left off and repeat the cycle. If we are working with RGBA pixels then only two pixels are needed to hide one byte of information.

Reading back the message is done in the reverse order. We start with the first color component and its least significant bit is used as the 8th bit in the byte we are extracting. Next color component contains the 7th bit and so on. After exactly 8 color components, we have successfully retrieved back one hidden byte.

© The Author(s), under exclusive licence to Springer Nature Switzerland AG 2018   57
B. Furht et al., *Digital Image Processing: Practical Approach*, SpringerBriefs in
Computer Science, https://doi.org/10.1007/978-3-319-96634-2_8

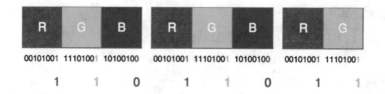

Fig. 8.1 Example of entering the message '11011011' into the RGB pixels by changing the least significant bit

Fig. 8.2 Adding the message (**a**) changing the least significant bit, (**b**) changing last 3 bits, (**c**) changing last 6 bits, and (**d**) changing all 8 bits

Using only one bit for hiding information is virtually impossible for the eye to detect the difference between the original image and the altered one. Through experimentation using up to 4 bits we have found that the images hardly change in most cases. Altering the first 4 bits of a color component adds or subtracts a maximum value of 8 and if only one bit is used, the value is either increased by one or stays the same.

Figure 8.2 shows the difference between images that had their first bits altered to hide the content of a file. The visual difference between the 1-bit image and 3-bit image is almost non-existent. In the 6-bit image, the image is severely altered by the file hiding process. Using 8-bits completely changes every color components value with the content of the file so entire original image is no longer visible.

The program in this chapter is the only console program example in the book. It gives the user the ability to control how many least significant bits to use to hide a secret file. The program flags are displayed below.

```
-p: 'image to pack into'
-u: 'image to unpack'
-f: 'file to read'
-o: 'output file'
-b: 'precision bits'
```

If we wish to hide the file "hideme.txt" in "image.png" using 3-bits and output the result image as "hidden.png", we use the following command:

```
pack -p image.png -f hideme.txt -o hidden.png -b 3
```

After the programs hides the text in the image, a new "hidden.png" file will be created in the directory that stores the new image. To extract back the file from the image, use the following command:

```
pack -u hidden.png -o extracted.txt
```

Any file, including other images, can be hid. However, if the length of the file to be hid exceeds the capacity of the image, then the message will be cut off at the point it exceeds the image capacity by the null byte terminator and a waring message will be displayed onto the screen to notify the user that only a certain amount of the message was able to be hid. As shown in program below, the length of the message is converted into kilobytes and is compared to the capacity of the image and how many bytes will be used from the image.

```
float len_kb = (float)len / 1024;//convert to kilobytes
float capacity = (float)(w * h * n * b) / (1024*8);
//how many bytes we need from image to pack data

float wrote = (len_kb < capacity ?  len_kb : capacity);
// to warn that the data we want to fide is to big compared to the image we // want
to hide it in and cut the message off with a NULL character

if (wrote == capacity) {
     printf("warning: '%s' is too large.\n", read_file);
     b64[(w * h * n * b / 8 )] = '\0';
}
```

Notice that image output is only in PNG format. This is because PNG utilizes lossless compression. As explained earlier in the book, lossless compression does not alter the pixel values so we can extract the original file we hid without any loss of data.

For the packing process to begin, we must first load the image and retrieve the pixel values using the stb library. Next, the content of the file that is to be hid is retrieved with fget(). At this point we can begin the packing process but there remains an issue we have not addressed yet. A hidden file's content may finish at any pixel in the image. When the hidden file is being extracted from the image, there is no indicator that signals the unpacking processes to stop. As it currently stands, once unpacking starts, it will read and extract data from every pixel. One obvious solution that may come to mind is stopping when a null byte terminator is read. This however won't work since binary files such as PDFs, the kind of files we may wish to hide, can contain zero bytes for other reasons then to end file streams. Essentially, any non-ASCII file may contain zero bytes in any part of the file so using a null byte terminator to terminate the unpacking process will result in only unpacking a part of the hidden file.

To fix this, using the same number of least significant bits as the hiding process, we can fill the values of the some of the first pixels to match the byte length of the file. Another solution, which we have chosen to implement, is converting the file into base64 form which works by splitting the data into 6-bit values so that the range of the new byte is between 0 and 63 as shown in Fig. 8.3. These 6-bit Base64 values are then replaced with an ASCII character as described in Table 8.1, so that any non-ASCII binary file can be converted a null terminated ASCII string.

Another issue is that the number of least significant bits needs to be incorporated inside the image so when the program is called upon to unpack the hidden file, the unpacking process can be made aware of how many least significant bits contain the hidden data. To solve this problem, the first three RGB components are used to store the number of bits used for packing as entered by the user. After base64 transformation of the file, the pack function can finally be called.

As shown in the program below, the first three color components in the first pixel are used to contain the number of least significant bits. Next, every color component following the first pixel has b many of its least significant bits cleared to zero. The innermost for loop ORs the component value with the correct bit from m to hide the data in the image. Once every bit in the messages' current byte is written, the pointer to the messages' content is incremented once to point to the next byte and the bit position is moved back to the 8th bit of the byte. This continues until the null terminator is reached.

01101000 01100101 01111001

011010 000110 010101 111001

Fig. 8.3 3 bytes are converted to 4 bytes by restricting the new bytes to 6 bits

Table 8.1 Base64 values converted to ASCII characters

Value	Char	Value	Char	Value	Char	Value	Char
0	A	16	Q	32	g	48	w
1	B	17	R	33	h	49	x
2	C	18	S	34	i	50	y
3	D	19	T	35	j	51	z
4	E	20	U	36	k	52	0
5	F	21	V	37	l	53	1
6	G	22	W	38	m	54	2
7	H	23	X	39	n	55	3
8	I	24	Y	40	o	56	4
9	J	25	Z	41	p	57	5
10	K	26	a	42	q	58	6
11	L	27	b	43	r	59	7
12	M	28	c	44	s	60	8
13	N	29	d	45	t	61	9
14	O	30	e	46	u	62	+
15	P	31	f	47	v	63	/

```
void pack(uint8* pixels, uint8* m, int w, int h, int n, int b)
{
    int bits = 7;
    int len = w * h * n;

    // first 3 color componets hold b value
    int i;
    for(i=0; i < 3; i++) {
        uint8* comp = pixels + i;
        *comp = bit_clear(*comp, 1, 1);
        *comp |= bit_range(b, i+1,1);
    }

    for(; i < len; i+=n) {

        for(int j=0; j < n; j++) {

            uint8* comp = pixels + i + j;
            *comp = bit_clear(*comp, b, b); // clear out first b bits

            for(int k=b-1; k >= 0; k--) {

                uint8 bit = *m & (1 << bits);

                *comp |= ((bit ? 1 : 0) << k);

                if (--bits == -1) {
                    bits = 7;
                    ++m;
                    if (*(m-1) == '\0')
                        return;
                }
            }
        }
    }
}
```

Unpacking follows similar steps but in reverse, as shown in the program below.

```
vector unpack(uint8* pixels, int w, int h, int n)
{
    vector b64; vector_init(&b64, sizeof(char), 1);
    uint8 c = 0;
    int bits = 7;
    int b = 0;

    int len = w * h * n;

    int i;
    for(i=0; i < 3; i++) {
        uint8* comp = pixels + i;
        b |= bit_range(*comp, 1, 1) << i;
    }
    if (!b)
        b = 8;

    for(; i < len; i+=n) {

        for(int j=0; j < n; j++) {

            uint8* comp = pixels + i + j;

            for(int k=b; k > 0; k--) {

                uint8 bit = bit_range(*comp, k, 1);
                c |= (bit << bits);

                if (--bits == -1) {
                    bits = 7;
                    if (c == '\0') goto done;
                    vector_push(&b64, &c);
                    c = 0;
                }
            }
        }
    }
    done: {
        char null = '\0';
        vector_push(&b64, &null);
        return b64;
    }
}
```

Like the packing function, the first three color components contain the number of least significant bits that the unpacking function will work with. Once b is determined, the innermost loop begins the byte reconstruction from b many bits from each color component. When a byte is fully extracted, it is recorded and bit position of the byte is reset back to the 8th bit. Once a null terminating byte is read, the function returns the vector containing the hidden content. The vector is a C++ inspired dynamic array. Since this program is written in C and C++ containers in the standard library are unavailable, we decided to write our own dynamic array. The implementation is available in vector.h in the main library folder. The returned content is then converted to the original file by reversing the base64 transformation using the b64toa () function. Next, the output is saved to disk using the output file name provided by the user in the form of flag and the program exists.

In this chapter, we have shown how to hide a file into an image by overwriting bits of the pixels and how to unpack that data into a separate data file by. In the process, we have also shown how to convert a data stream into base64 form. Next, we focus on transition animations between two images.

Chapter 9
Image Transition

In slideshow applications or video editors that are transition animations that reveal the next slide or image in various visual styles which may include fading in and out between the two images. The focus of this chapter is the transition from one image to another over time as can be seen in Fig. 9.2. Transition animations are applied over a period of time to both images and each pixel to be displayed is altered slightly each instance depending on a function of time. For animating a linear transition between images where one image turns into a different image, we use the following formula where each pixel value is determined by a transition time point t whose range is between 0 and 1:

$$r = bt + a(t - 1)$$

The variables are defined as: r is the resultant pixel value, a is pixel from image A, b is a pixel from image B, and t is the transition variable. This transition function is linear as in time variable t linearly controls the amount of reveal of image B over A.

In this project setup, there are three buttons and one slider bar. Two buttons are used for selecting the images, one for image A and one for image B. The third button is for saving the resultant image that is displayed in the middle. The resultant image is determined by the slider bar which controls the transition factor t. Once the two images are selected, moving the slider will change the transition value and generate a new image that blends the two images. The weight of each image on the resultant image is determined by the transition value.

When the transition value is 0 in the equation, the generated image is a replica of the first image. Similarly, when the transition value is 1 in the equation, the resultant image is a replica of the second image, thus completing the transition. Essentially, when t is closer to 0, the first image is predominant in the mix. When t passes 0.5 on the slider bar, the second image becomes more predominant in the blend. The more predominant an image is, the greater weight it holds on the view of the resultant image. When the transition bar is precisely at point 0.5, then both images are equally weighted, as shown in Fig. 9.1.

© The Author(s), under exclusive licence to Springer Nature Switzerland AG 2018   65
B. Furht et al., *Digital Image Processing: Practical Approach*, SpringerBriefs in
Computer Science, https://doi.org/10.1007/978-3-319-96634-2_9

Fig. 9.1 Example of transition from face 1 to face 2, t = 0.5

Fig. 9.2 Image B is more saturated than Image A; it is revealed at t = 0.35 transition value

This, however, is not always true. If image B is more saturated than image A, then image B will be more visible over image A before the 0.5 point. This case is shown in Fig. 9.2.

Using the formula, the following function calculates and assigns the pixel value of the result image.

```
void image_transtition(uint8* pixels, Image a, Image b, float t)
{
    int length = a.width * a.height * RGBA;
    for(int i=0; i < length; i++)
        pixels[i] = (b.pixels[i] * t) + (a.pixels[i] * (1 - t));
}
```

Notice that the formula is applied to each pixel as the loop iterates over each pixel of the two images. The length of the loop is determined by multiplying the width, height of one of the images time and the number of channels which results in total amount of bytes of the image. The loop then iterates over each color component and assigns the proper value determined by the function.

Observe that the program does not allow two images of different sizes. The program assumes that the two images are the same for the following reasons: there is no conditional statement to properly prevent two images of varied sizes to be inserted and there is no resizing procedure performed before the transition function is called to allow two images of varied sizes to be used. The ability to use varied sizes is left as an exercise. We discuss image resizing thoroughly in the "Image to Image Embedding" chapter and you can embed the resizing function used in that chapter into this demo program.

```
// if new a and new b are loaded
if (a.texture_loaded && b.texture_loaded) {

    // r is not created
    if (!r.texture_loaded) {
        r.width = a.width;
        r.height = a.height;
        r.pixels = (uint8*)malloc(a.width * a.height * RGBA);
        image_transtition(r.pixels, a, b, t);
        texture_image(&r);
    }

    // t is moved
    else if (prev_t != t) {
        reset_texture(&r);
        prev_t = t;
        image_transtition(r.pixels, a, b, t);
        texture_image(&r);
    }
}
```

After the user selects two new images, enough memory is allocated for the new resultant image. The pointer to that new memory is passed to image transition function. Then, a new texture for the resultant image is created which gets rendered outside of the if statement. When the slider is moved, old texture of the resultant image is destroyed, the image transition function is called, and a new texture is created for the new image. The following code below deletes the old texture of the resultant image and overwrite Notice when slider is moved, the value for t is updated, so detecting slider change is done by comparing the old slider value from the previous iteration with the new value.

A save button is another feature of this program which showcases the use of the stb library's ability to save an image from a pointer of pixel values. As shown below, the name of the saved image is t times 100 which gets saved to sname. Next, the image is saved to the project folder with the stbi_write_png function.

```
// display texture
if (r.texture_loaded) {
  ImGui::Image((void*)r.texture, resize_ui(r.width, r.height), ImVec2(0,0),
        ImVec2(1,1), ImVec4(1,1,1,1), ImVec4(0,255,0,255));

  if (ImGui::Button("Save")) {
    char sname[1000];
    sprintf(sname, "%d.png", (int)(t*100));
    stbi_write_png(sname, a.width, a.height, 4, r.pixels, 0);
  }
}
```

The formula we used is a simple linear function but more complex transition functions can be implemented. Some example are *ease, ease-in, ease-out* which are CSS animation functions implemented in popular web browsers We leave the coding of these functions as exercise, but only a few changes to the image_ transtition function are necessary to implement them.

9.1   Compiler Optimizations

In the makefile located in the directory of this project, the OPT compiler flag controls the optimization level for the compiler. In gcc, there are four different levels of optimization that range between 0 and 3. The use of optimization does not alter the behavior of the program but forces the compiler to produce a program that may run faster and more efficiently by using clever compiler tricks such as finding ways to reduce the number of instructions, using more efficient instruction in place of slower ones, etc. Generally, speedup of the program between the levels is noticeable during program execution, but we can visually see the change in the assembly output of different optimization levels. With -S flag, gcc will output assembly code for the C++ files we've included. To produce the assembly output, we run this command in the console:

```
make asm
```

We have also included two files titled "image_transition_O0.s" that contains the assembly output for the transition function with the lowest optimization level (-O0) and "image_transition_O3.s" that contains the assembly with the optimization turned all the way up to level three. The difference we want to highlight is the heavy use of SIMD (Single Instruction, Multiple Data) instructions in the optimized version. Normal instructions move a single piece of data to a CPU register, perform some operation, and return the result, which can be inefficient and slow compared to SIMD instructions that concurrently perform the same operation on multiple pieces of data, increasing the speed of execution and making the program run more efficiently.

Inside the loop of the transition function, there are 3 basic operations: subtraction, multiplication, and addition. Since each piece of data is a single byte, the SIMD instructions pack multiple pixels worth of bytes into larger 128-bit registers instead of the general single-instruction 32-bit registers. In the register, the SIMD instructions perform the required operations to multiple pixels and assign the packed result back into to the heap memory. Since multimedia applications generally perform a lot of computation, SIMD instructions can improve program performance tremendously.

In this chapter, we have discussed and implemented a simple linear transition function between two images using a slider representing the time variable **t**. We leave you to implement other transition functions that are not linear. We also explained briefly how multimedia application can benefit from special SIMD instructions. In the next chapter, we discuss image resizing and embedding.

Chapter 10
Image-to-Image Embedding

In this chapter we present a program in which the user can embed an image onto another image. The user selects two images, one used as the background, and one to place on top, and can select wherever on the background image to place the second image. As shown in Fig. 10.1, we can select a background image, in this case a TV in Times Square, and embed another image onto it, in this case a playful red panda. The program also features the ability to resize the overlay image.

Embedding a new image is as simple as replacing the pixels of the background image with the pixels of the new overlay image starting at the first row and column of where the user clicked on the background image. However, before we start copying over pixels, there is one extra step we must do. To be able display large image on the UI, images are displayed with a maximum size of 350 pixels for width and height dimensions. You might have noticed this in the previous demo programs appear in this form:

```
#define MAX_SIDE 350
ImGui::Image((void*)a.texture, resize_ui(a.width, a.height, MAX_SIDE));
```

where resize_ui returns an ImGui vector with the dimensions of the image resized to the maximum allowed size while maintaining aspect ratio. As a result, when the user clicks on a location, the x and y coordinates of the location must be translated to the actual location of the pixel in the image. Assume that a 700×700 background image, which gets displayed as a 350×350 image by ImGui, is clicked on the center. ImGui then reports that the x and y coordinates of the clicked location is 175 and 175 respectively. Translating these coordinates to the pixel in the image results in the pixel at coordinates 350 and 350. The pixels of the overlay image can now be copied over starting with the background pixel in row 350 and column 350.

© The Author(s), under exclusive licence to Springer Nature Switzerland AG 2018   71
B. Furht et al., *Digital Image Processing: Practical Approach*, SpringerBriefs in
Computer Science, https://doi.org/10.1007/978-3-319-96634-2_10

Fig. 10.1 The user can select a background image and embed another image after resizing by clicking anywhere on the middle image

```
ImVec2 canvas_pos = ImGui::GetCursorScreenPos();
ImGui::ImageButton((void*)r.texture, resize_ui(r.width, r.height, MAX_SIDE),
    ImVec2(0,0), ImVec2(1,1), 0, ImVec4(0,0,0,0), ImVec4(1,1,1,1));


if (ImGui::IsItemHovered()) {
    if (ImGui::IsMouseClicked(0)) {
        ImVec2 pos =  ImVec2(ImGui::GetIO().MousePos.x - canvas_pos.x,
            ImGui::GetIO().MousePos.y - canvas_pos.y);
        embed(&a, &b, &r, pos); //embeds pasded on new postion
    }
}
```

When the user clicks on a position on the background image (center image in the UI), the coordinates are sent off to the embed function. The function's parameters are the struct of the background image, the struct of the overlay image, the struct for the final resultant image after embedding, and the location of the mouse click on the background image.

```
// embed image b on a at location pos
void embed(Image* a, Image* b, Image* r, ImVec2 pos)
{
    // allocate memory for r and copy a's pixels
    reset_image(r);
    r->width = a->width;
    r->height = a->height;
    r->pixels = (uint8*)malloc(r->width * r->height * RGBA);
    memcpy(r->pixels, a->pixels, r->width * r->height * RGBA);

    // calculate ratio of the ui size to actual size of r
    // to translate pos to a pixel in r
    ImVec2 ui_size = resize_ui(r->width, r->height, MAX_SIDE);
    ImVec2 ratio (r->width / ui_size.x, r->height / ui_size.y);

    // row counter of image r
    int y_r = ratio.y * pos.y;

    for(int y_b = 0; y_r < r->height && y_b < b->height; y_r++, y_b++) {
```

```
        // pointers for the current row on r and b
        uint8* r_row =   r->pixels + (y_r * r->width * RGBA);
        uint8* b_row =   b->pixels + (y_b * b->width * RGBA);

        // column counter of image r
        int x_r = ratio.x * pos.x;

        for(int x_b = 0; x_r < r->width && x_b < b->width; x_r++, x_b++) {

            // pointers for the current column of r and b
            uint8* r_pixel = r_row + (x_r * RGBA);
            uint8* b_pixel = b_row + (x_b * RGBA);

            r_pixel[0] = b_pixel[0]; //R
            r_pixel[1] = b_pixel[1]; //G
            r_pixel[2] = b_pixel[2]; //B
            r_pixel[3] = b_pixel[3]; //A
        }
    }
    texture_image(r);
}
```

At the top of the embed function, memory is allocated for the resultant image and the pixel values of the background image is copied over. Next the coordinates of pos are translated to the row and column on the background in the form of y_r and x_r variables. The outer and inner loop keep track of the row and column counters of both the background image and the overlay image and with some pointer arithmetic the pixel values of the overlay image is assigned to the pixels of the background image.

Resizing is done by the user in the textbox area under the overlay image. In our implementation, downsizing a dimension is done by downsampling pixels from the original as dictated by the ratio of the original image size over the new size. Downsampling is done by skipping certain rows and columns of the original image while copying the original pixel values to the new image during the resizing process. Upsizing is done by repeating certain rows and columns as dictated by the ratio.

Which pixels to downsample or repeat for the resized image is determined by calculating the width and height ratios between the images using this definition:

$$width_{ratio} = \frac{original_{width}}{new_{width}}, \quad height_{ratio} = \frac{original_{height}}{new_{height}}$$

Let's work with an example. To downsample a 200×400 image to 100×200, the ratio is two for both width and height so we drop every second row and column from the original during resizing. To visually see how this works, please refer to Fig. 10.2

The mechanics behind enlarging an image is similar. We first determine the width and height ratios, but this time we get ratio values that are less than one since the new image size is larger. Following the same procedure in Fig. 10.2, we determine which pixels to repeat by diving each x and y coordinates of the pixels of the new image

Fig. 10.2 A 3 × 3 image is resized to 2 × 2 by downsampling rows and columns using the ratio between the two

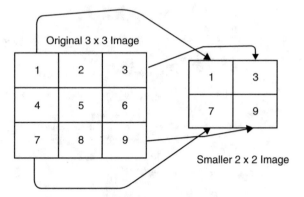

pixels with the width and height ratios and using the pixels from the original image with these coordinates. You can see this in effect in Fig. 10.3.

Note that in the case that the new width is bigger than the original but the height is smaller or vice versa, we compute the x and y coordinates the same way using the ratios. If the new width is bigger, the ratio will be less than one so repetition in the columns from the original image will occur. As the new height is smaller and the height ratio is greater than 1, downsampling will be applied to the rows of the original image.

```c
void resize_image(Image* img, int new_w, int new_h)
{
    uint8* resized_img_pixels = (uint8*)malloc(new_w * new_h * RGBA);

    float w_ratio = (float)new_w / img->width;
    float h_ratio = (float)new_h / img->height;

    for (int y=0; y < new_h; y++) {

        uint8* row = resized_img_pixels + (y * new_w * RGBA);
        uint8* original = img->pixels + ( (int)(y / h_ratio ) * img->width * RGBA);

        for (int x=0; x < new_w; x++) {

            uint8* pixel = row + (x * RGBA);
            uint8* original_pixel = original + ( (int)(x / w_ratio) * RGBA);

            pixel[0] = original_pixel[0]; //R
            pixel[1] = original_pixel[1]; //G
            pixel[2] = original_pixel[2]; //B
            pixel[3] = original_pixel[3]; //A
        }
    }
}
```

The resize function accepts the struct of the original image and the new width and height dimensions. At the top memory is allocated for the new image and the width and height ratios are calculated. The outer and inner loop iterate over each row and column of the new image, and using the ratios, which pixel to copy over from the original image is calculated.

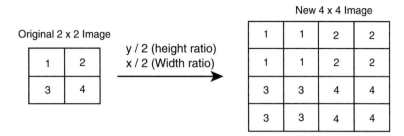

Fig. 10.3 Upsizing is done by repeating pixel values in the new image from the original image. Repetition amount in the rows and columns is dictated by the ratio

There are of course many other techniques for resizing images. Some involve taking the average of the neighboring pixels when down and up sampling, and there are other more complex interpolation methods so we leave that to you to research on your own once you've mastered the basics of resizing as explained in this chapter.

Chapter 11
Changing Color of Selected Objects

The project for this chapter was completed by the FAU student Mila Manastasova as part of the Introduction to Image and Video Processing class at Florida Atlantic University taught in Spring 2018.

The objective of the project was to design a program and user interface, which will change some predetermined colors to another color (please refer to Figs. 11.1 and 11.2). If any pixels are white, a region of 20×20 around the white pixel is changed to an alternating pattern of blue and pink. In the case that the pixel is red, the pixel is changed to blue. Essentially the program showcases the 'selection by color' tool available in popular image editing software. Starting at this point, the rest of the chapter is the student's report.

11.1 Implementation Description

The implementation involves different steps in order to accomplish all the requirements. First of all, the main window has to be created.

```
GLFWwindow* window = glfwCreateWindow(1000, 700, "Project 1", NULL, NULL);
glfwMakeContextCurrent(window);
```

A constructor for the window is created containing all its parameters as an input value. The first two parameters correspond to the width and the height of the desired window. As third parameter we insert the name of the main window. After all the necessary parameters are defined, a function that creates the window with the inserted values is invoked. A color for the background of the main window is set using a special vector structure.

© The Author(s), under exclusive licence to Springer Nature Switzerland AG 2018
B. Furht et al., *Digital Image Processing: Practical Approach*, SpringerBriefs in
Computer Science, https://doi.org/10.1007/978-3-319-96634-2_11

Fig. 11.1 The original image is loaded and presented on the screen (when START button is pressed)

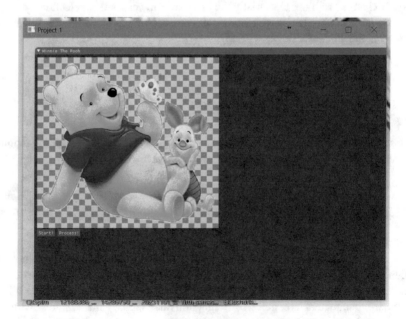

Fig. 11.2 The program changes the background and the color of the sweater (when PROCESS button is pressed)

An infinite "while" loop is created so that the program runs until the user closes it and forces the program to stop. Inside the loop the characteristics of the next window – the window created in the next iteration of the loop. An inner window is created. The user can change the size of it, minimize it, and to press all the buttons. All these actions are immediately provoking the change of the window and in the next iteration the newly created window is different.

For the first functionality of the program – load an image from the database in the computer and show it on the screen, a button named "Start!" is created. When pressing the button an image called "pooh1.jpg" is loaded into the structure "a" of Image type. The function stbi_load("name.jpg", &image.width, &image.height, &image.n, RGBA) automatically puts all the information of the loaded image inside the attributes of the Image. The width, the height, the number of components per pixel and order of the components are accessible from now.

To show the content of the image that is now loaded in the memory and is also in the Image structure "a", a function texture_image(&a) is called passing pointer to the first pixel of the image. This ends the implementation of the first part of the project and the functionality of the first button.

The second functionality requires change of the components of the pixels. This part is not restrictive, and any algorithm can be applied in order to create a new image or to change the features of the loaded one. Pressing a button called "Process!" is placed next to the button "Start!". Once this button is pressed the image content is changed and the changes are immediately displayed on the screen.

The algorithm used for this program involves change of the background and of particular parts of the image. First of all, all the image has to be traverse. As the image inside the memory is just a sequence of bits, but for the users it is a matrix – has rows and columns, all the loops allow the usage of only one counting variable but also allow the implementation using two counters – one for the rows and one for the columns.

Some auxiliary variables are declared at the beginning – "inBlue" is a boolean variable that indicates if a given section, currently accessed, is blue or not blue – purple. A variable count is used to count the number of passed rows, so that later we can make changes when some certain number of rows is reached. The number of bytes per pixel is stored in a variable called "bytesPerPixel" and the number of bytes per row is also stored in a variable called "bytesPerRow".

The first "for" loop is passing through all the rows. This means the all the position of a row will be accessed before going to the next row. This implementation requires another "for" loop nested to this one so that all the columns can be accessed in each row. However, the number of the passed rows is checked. If the numbers of rows passed is twenty, the counter is set again to zero and the" inBlue" variable is set to its opposite. This allows to change the starting color for each 20 rows – 20 rows will start being blue, then 20 will start being purple and so on.

The second loop is accessing each 20th pixel of each row. This is how the usage of counter can be avoided. The check of the "inBlue" is made again so that the columns are alternating as well. The combination of both loops and the conditions for the color and the counter of the rows and columns allow to make a chess board pattern.

In order to change only some part of the image – only the background, the values of each component of a pixel are checked. If all of them are higher than 250, the color is changed. To access all the pixels of a column, another "for" loop is created going only from 0 to 20. Then the components we want to access are reached by a. pixels[((row)* bytesPerRow + (col * bytesPerPixel)) + (0;1;2;3) + i * 4]. To pass all the image that has been already processed, first the number of rows passed is multiplied by the number of bytes per row. The number of columns passed is multiplied by the bytes per pixel and both are added. The column for loop is skipping 20 rows and another loop using i is implemented, so the value of i*bytesPerPixel has to be added. That is the approach to get to every pixel of the image.

Nevertheless, every pixel is composed of 4 components – 4 bytes. To reach all of them, a number between 0 and 3 is added, where 0 is for the red component byte, 1 is for the green, 2 is for the blue and 3 is for the alpha component. Changing the values of the component bytes changes the color of the pixel.

Besides changing the background, a particular part of the image is modified as well when the "process!" button is pressed. The T-shirt of Winnie the pooh is changes its color.

First of all, the color of the currently accessed pixel is checked and it will be changed only if it is red – the color of the T-shirt. As there may be more red elements in the image, the zone of the change is reduced only from 1/3 to 2.2/3 of the height and from 1/3 to 2.4/3 from the width. Only when we are inside this zone the color red will be modified. If this is the case the red component of the image will be exchanges with the blue using auxiliary variable. In this way the shades of the image are not going to be changed but the color is going to be different. The same algorithm is implemented in the else part of the if statement when the pointer points to part that is going to become purple.

At the end the memory of the image is freed, the window is rendered and in case if exit of the program the window is shut down.

The program can be found in the repository GitHub.

Chapter 12
Loading and Inserting Objects in an Image

The project aims to use the ImGui libraries to create a program with friendly user interface. The project was completed by the FAU student Mila Manastasova as part of the Introduction to Image and Video Processing class at Florida Atlantic University taught in Spring 2018.

The main objective is to allow the selection of various images from the database, load them into image structures, and randomly place the second (furniture) inside the first (apartment plan) in a place that is not yet occupied by another furniture or a wall. After the design program has been executed, the customer may save the apartment image. This project follows Chap. 10, which deals with embedding a small image into a bigger image.

The implementation involves different steps to accomplish all the requirements. For the first functionality of the program – load an image from the database in the computer and show it on the screen, a button named "Select Apartment!" is created. When pressing the button, a drop menu is shown, and the user has to choose a picture from the database. This picture is loaded into image structure. The choice of the second picture is similar. One the image of the furniture is loaded the user can resize the image or to use its original size. When both pictures are loaded two new buttons appear on the screen.

"Place furniture" is copying the second picture inside the first one in a random place. For this purpose, a random point must be created. The X coordinate point must be somewhere between the left top corner to the right corner – the width of A, minus the width of the image B so that the furniture image can be places inside the apartment image without exceeding the limits of the big image. The same method is used for the Y coordinate of the point – it may be from the top of the image A until the height of image A minus the height of image B. The starting point is then calculated as the multiplication of the width of the image A – the length of the row, and the Y coordinate of the point, in order to place the picture B in the chosen row. Then the X coordinate is summed to the current result to place the picture somewhere inside the width of the A image.

© The Author(s), under exclusive licence to Springer Nature Switzerland AG 2018
B. Furht et al., *Digital Image Processing: Practical Approach*, SpringerBriefs in
Computer Science, https://doi.org/10.1007/978-3-319-96634-2_12

To place the image first a check must be performed. If the randomly chosen place is free (there are no black lines – walls, other pieces of furniture, doors, windows, etc.), the image B is going to be placed in image A with starting position the randomly calculated point. To place the small image inside the big one a loop going through all the components from the small image is required, copying the values of the pixels of B to the pixels of A to the given location in A. To place the small image in a consecutive way inside the big one every time the counter of the loop is divisible by the width of the small picture multiplied by the 4 RGBA components, the row has to be switched. The value of the big image width minus the small picture's width is added to the loop counter variable when accessing the big picture. That is how every new row inside the small picture will also result in a new row inside the big picture. Finally, the position of the starting point must be also added to the counter value of the loop when accessing the big image so that the copying process starts from the random point. All these steps are performed inside the function insert:

```
extern "C" void insert(Image a, Image b){}
```

The user may choose up to 10 pieces of furniture as long as they fit – less than 100 random points are generated to find a location where the furniture can be placed. If more than 100 random points are created and the furniture still does not fit, the program displays a text message announcing that the apartment is full. After a piece of furniture is chosen and placed in the apartment plan, the user may see the new design and a list of all the chosen furniture and their names. If the user likes the design s/he can save the image in the database and then apply the design to his/her real home (Figs. 12.1, 12.2 and 12.3).

Fig. 12.1 The snapshot of the drop-down menu to select the images

The program can be found in the repository GitHub.

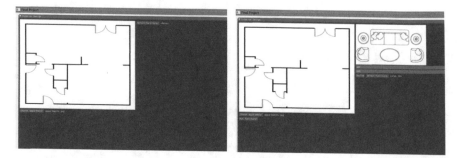

Fig. 12.2 Loading image of the apartment and the image of the furniture. Resizing the image of the furniture

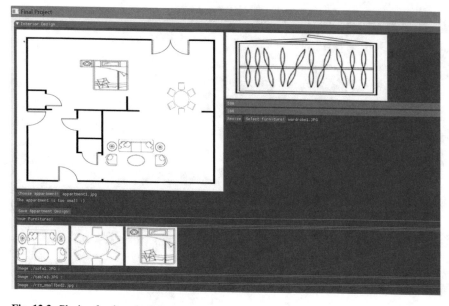

Fig. 12.3 Placing furniture in the apartment

Chapter 13
Swap Faces in an Image

The project was completed by the FAU student Connor as part of the Introduction to Image and Video Processing class at Florida Atlantic University taught in Spring 2018.

The face swap project is composed of three tasks: (1) load the image, (2) detect the faces, and (3) swap these faces. The task of loading images has already been discussed in the book. In this project, we select an image with two faces and the program detects the faces and swap them.

13.1 Rapid Object Detection Using a Boosted Cascade of Simple Features

In this project, we implemented the OpenCV Haar Feature-based Cascade Classifier for frontal faces. This is an old algorithm, originally published in 2001 by Paul Viola and Michael Jones. Many algorithms had existed prior to the Viola-Jones algorithm that focused on extracting features from images using various feature selection techniques. Additionally, there are many popular feature selection methods such as HOG, (Histogram of Oriented Gradients) and LBP (Local Binary Patterns) that have all shown great results for this kind of applications. The Viola-Jones algorithm presents three key contributions to object detection: (1) use of the integral image for quickly computing features, (2) the AdaBoost algorithm to select a subset of critical features and train a classifier, and (3) a cascade of classifiers to reduce the search space of locations where faces are likely to be. Figure 13.1 illustrates traditional machine learning approach and deep learning approach.

© The Author(s), under exclusive licence to Springer Nature Switzerland AG 2018
B. Furht et al., *Digital Image Processing: Practical Approach*, SpringerBriefs in Computer Science, https://doi.org/10.1007/978-3-319-96634-2_13

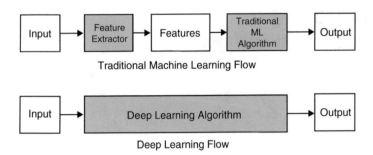

Fig. 13.1 Traditional machine learning versus deep learning flow

13.2   Features in Images

When describing a car, you might describe it with features such as year, brand, wheel count, etc. However, the features used to describe images follow different format. Features discussed in this chapter belong to one of three classes, 2-rectangle, 3-rectangle, and 4-rectangle features. Figure 13.2 shows some examples of these features. Example in A and B illustrate all possible 2-rectangle features, while many more possibilities of 3- and 4-rectangle features such as C and D exist. These rectangular features are not a complete representation of all possible patterns that can be discovered in these images, however they are very useful for simple image structure.

13.3   Integral Image

The primary purpose of the integral image representation is to save computational cost on computing the features discussed above in image sub-windows. Confusion matrix, shown in Fig. 13.3, is very important for understanding the technique proposed by Viola Jones. There are many metrics that are used to describe the performance of a binary classifier. In our case, the cascade classifier must determine which regions are likely to contain a face and which are not. In this example, a false positive, (also known as Type II error), is a rectangle outlining a region that does not contain a face. A false negative, (also known as Type I error), is when the classifier fails to recognize a face altogether. The goal of an optimal classifier is to have these two errors as close to each other as possible with the case of interest, (usually Type II), as low as possible.

Different False Positive Rates (FPR) and False Negative Rates (FNR) are achieved by varying the little c in the following equation:

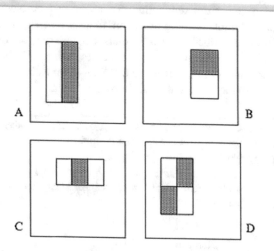

Fig. 13.2 Examples of features in an image (**a**) and (**b**) 2-rectangle features, (**c**) 3-rectangle features, (**d**) 4-rectangle features

Fig. 13.3 Confusion matrix

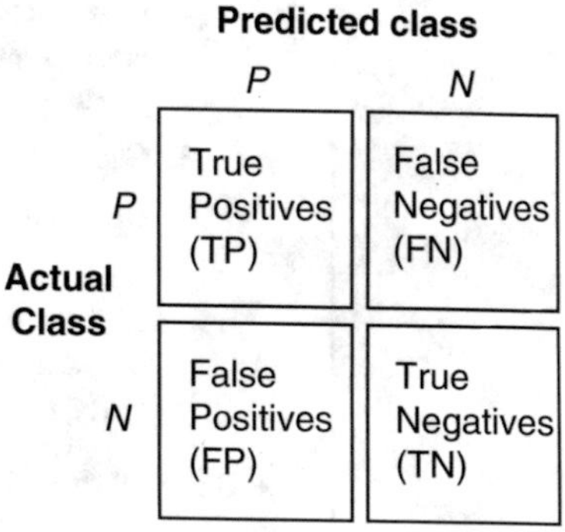

		Predicted class	
		P	N
Actual Class	P	True Positives (TP)	False Negatives (FN)
	N	False Positives (FP)	True Negatives (TN)

$$
Class(x_i) = \left\{ \begin{array}{ll} G_1 & \text{if} \dfrac{f_1(x_i)}{f_2(x_i)} \geq c \\ G_2 & \text{otherwise} \end{array} \right\}
$$

In early stages of the classifier it is important to minimize the false negative rate because we do not want to risk missing any potential regions with faces early on, however, as the classifier progresses, the false positive rate becomes more important.

The Viola Jones algorithm has a very important constraint, it must run in real-time. Therefore, computing massive parametric models can become a bottleneck that prevents the algorithm from doing this. To solve this problem, the AdaBoost classifier uses an ensemble learning procedure to learn a series of simple classifiers. These classifiers are described as weak learners, because they are only a little better than simply taking random guesses at the classes. These classifiers are decision stumps, this simple algorithm decides the class based on a single feature. Below is the formal procedure for training the AdaBoost classifier:

- Given example images $(x_1, y_1), \ldots, (x_n, y_n)$ where $y_i = 0, 1$ for negative and positive examples respectively.

- Initialize weights $w_{1,i} = \frac{1}{2m}, \frac{1}{2l}$ for $y_i = 0, 1$ respectively, where m and l are the number of negatives and positives respectively.

- For $t = 1, \ldots, T$:

  1. Normalize the weights,

  $$w_{t,i} \leftarrow \frac{w_{t,i}}{\sum_{j=1}^{n} w_{t,j}}$$

  so that w_t is a probability distribution.

  2. For each feature, j, train a classifier h_j which is restricted to using a single feature. The error is evaluated with respect to w_t, $\epsilon_j = \sum_i w_i |h_j(x_i) - y_i|$.

  3. Choose the classifier, h_t, with the lowest error ϵ_t.

  4. Update the weights:

  $$w_{t+1,i} = w_{t,i}\beta_t^{1-e_i}$$

  where $e_i = 0$ if example x_i is classified correctly, $e_i = 1$ otherwise, and $\beta_t = \frac{\epsilon_t}{1-\epsilon_t}$.

- The final strong classifier is:

$$h(x) = \begin{cases} 1 & \sum_{t=1}^{T} \alpha_t h_t(x) \geq \frac{1}{2} \sum_{t=1}^{T} \alpha_t \\ 0 & \text{otherwise} \end{cases}$$

where $\alpha_t = \log \frac{1}{\beta_t}$

The AdaBoost classifier also works as a feature selection technique in the Viola Jones algorithm. By combining weak classifiers, we are able to dramatically reduce the number of features used and save the computational cost that would be required from another parametric model such as Support Vector Machine.

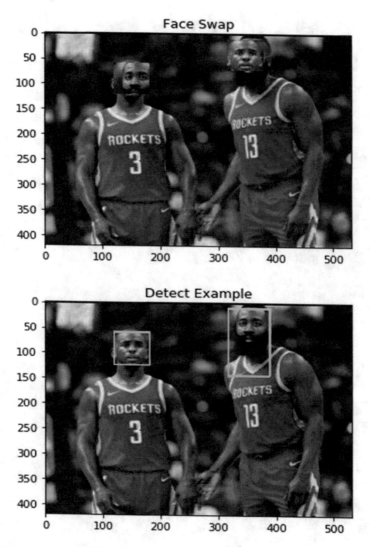

Fig. 13.4 Example of swapping face

The cascade classifier is the strategy used by this algorithm to progressively reduce the search space where potential faces are. This is done through a series of classifiers increasing in the number of features evaluated. According to the paper from Viola-Jones, the purpose of this is "to reduce by over one half the number of locations where the final detector must be evaluated". This is another trick to speed up the computational bottleneck and achieve real-time performance. Program code and example of swapping faces are shown below (Fig. 13.4).

```
# Libraries needed for program
import cv2
import numpy as np
import matplotlib.pyplot as plt


#Detect the Faces
'''
Function takes in the grayscale version of the image, returns a matrix
containing all faces in the format -- [x y w h] with x, y refering to the
top left point of the rectangle bounding the correspond face
'''
def detect(gray):
    #Load frontal face features from xml file (previously trained)
    face_cascade = cv2.CascadeClassifier('haarcascade_frontalface_default.xml')
    faces = face_cascade.detectMultiScale(gray, 1.3, 5)
    return faces

#Draw Rectangles
def drawRectangles(frame, faces):
    for (x, y, w, h) in faces: #Loop through each face
        cv2.rectangle(frame, (x,y), (x+w, h+h), (255, 255, 0), 2)
        #Parameters of function (image, top left coordinates, bottom right coordinate
        # color of rectangle, thickness of rectangle)

#Swap the pixels in the detected rectangles, (thus swapping faces)
def swap(frame, faces):
    Paul = faces[0]
    Harden = faces[1]
    for x in range(59, 121):
        for y in range(120, 182):
            #Have to pass value by copy to make swap
            temp = [ frame[x][y][0], frame[x][y][1], frame[x][y][2] ]
            #3 color channels(RGB), this is why we access [0],[1], and [2] of the image
            frame[x][y] = frame[x-48][y+197]
            frame[x-48][y+197] = temp
    return frame

image = cv2.imread('./images/PaulHarden.jpg')
gray = cv2.cvtColor(image, cv2.COLOR_BGR2GRAY) # Do some color transformations
faces = detect(gray)
canvas = swap(image, faces)
b,g,r = cv2.split(canvas)
canvas = cv2.merge([r,g,b])
plt.imshow(canvas)
plt.title('Face Swap')
plt.show()

#Detect Example
detectImage = cv2.imread('./images/PaulHarden.jpg')
gray = cv2.cvtColor(detectImage, cv2.COLOR_BGR2GRAY)
faces = detect(gray)
drawRectangles(detectImage, faces)
b,g,r = cv2.split(detectImage)
detectImage = cv2.merge([r,g,b])
plt.imshow(detectImage)
plt.title('Detect Example')
plt.show()
```